Living Expectantly

Living
EXPECTANTLY

BRIAN L. HARBOUR

BROADMAN PRESS
NASHVILLE, TENNESSEE

ISBN: 0-8054-1544-0
Dewey Decimal Classification: 226.6
Subject Headings: BIBLE. N.T. ACTS
Library of Congress Catalog Number: 89-49669

Printed in the United States of America

Library of Congress Cataloging-in-Publication Data
Harbour, Brian L.
    Living expectantly / Brian L. Harbour
        p.   cm. -- (Living the New Testament faith)
    Includes bibliographical references.
    ISBN 0-8054-1544-0
    1. Bible. N.T. Acts--Commentaries. I. Title. II. Series
BS2595.3.H34 1990
226.6'07--dc20

                                                                89-49669
                                                                CIP

Contents

Preface

The man lived with his wife on the old family farm for years, barely scratching out a living. All the while, beneath the barren, dusty, almost uncultivatable land was a rich supply of oil. While digging a water well, the farmer discovered this. Thus, he and his wife enjoyed a life of rich blessings. The farmer said, "And to think, we lived here all these years without knowing how rich we were!"

Many Christians are like that farmer. They go through their days, barely hanging on in their spiritual lives, living in their own weak ways; while beneath the surface, the power of God is ready to break forth in their lives. Most Christians don't know how rich they are.

As we study the story of the early church that Luke told us about in the Book of Acts, we discover those first Christians were a lot like us. They quarreled and became discouraged. They often misunderstood the scope of God's love, and they yielded to temptation. But the one difference between them and us is this: They lived with a sense of expectancy. They were like the little girl listening to her grandmother reading stories from the Bible, and her grandmother asked her what she thought of it. The little girl responded, "Oh, I love it. You never know what God is going to do next!"

God is at work now as He was then. He wants to explode the possibilities of our lives as He did theirs. My prayer is that you read this book on the exciting story of the establishment and development of the Christian church and learn to *live expectantly*.

1 Laying the Foundation

Acts 1:1—2:13

Thomas J. Altizer, William Hamilton, and Paul Van Buren spawned a theological thunderstorm several years ago when they declared, "God is dead." In the midst of the debates which headlined national news magazines and polarized theological institutions, one church put this message on their outdoor sign: "God is alive and well, visiting hours every Sunday."

If any document ever affirmed God is alive and well, it is the Book of Acts. Acts is not only the pivotal book of the New Testament. It is also the primary document which describes the exciting development of the New Testament Church. The fifth book in the New Testament corpus is the Book of Acts. But the acts of whom?

Since the middle of the second century, the book has been known as the "Acts of the Apostles." After chapter 12, however, little mention is made of any of the original apostles.

Others have declared this book to be the "Acts of the Holy Spirit." While it is true that reference is made to the Holy Spirit over fifty times in Acts, eleven chapters of the book do not mention the Holy Spirit at all.

To whose acts does the title refer? Luke gives us the answer in the opening verse of the book: "The first account I composed, Theophilus, about all that *Jesus* began to do and teach" (Acts 1:1, author's italics). In the Gospels, we see what Jesus began to do until the day He was taken up to be at the right hand of the Father. In Acts, we see what He continued to do in His church through the aid of the Holy Spirit in the lives of the apostles and other believers. This book, then, in the strictest sense, is a book about the acts of the resurrected Lord.

The first act of the resurrected Lord was to prepare the apostles for the task before them and lay the foundation for their work. They were to be His witnesses "in Jerusalem, and in all Judea and Samaria, and even to the remotest part of the earth" (Acts 1:8). What did they need to carry out this assignment?

Evidence (1:1-3)

First of all, the apostles needed evidence. Before they turned their backs on their former lives and committed themselves to sharing the gospel, they needed the assurance that the gospel was true, that Jesus had defeated death, and that He really was the Son of God. The resurrected Lord gave them that evidence. Luke told us in verse 3: "To these He also presented Himself alive, after His suffering, by many convincing proofs, appearing to them over a period of forty days" (1:3). The Greek word for "proofs" *(tekmeriois)* is a strong word. The *Amplified Bible* catches the scope of it by translating the verse like this: "By [a series of] many convincing demonstrations—unquestionable evidence and infallible proofs." In those forty days Jesus spent with the apostles, each of them became convinced beyond a shadow of a doubt that Jesus was the resurrected Lord.

What evidence did Jesus present? Both Paul in 1 Corinthians 15 and Luke in our text affirmed the primary evidence was the appearances of Jesus. Jesus came to the apostles, ate with them, and fellowshiped with them. He showed Himself to them alive. The appearances of Jesus were unquestionable evidence and infallible proof that Jesus had been raised from the dead and that He was indeed the Son of God. That fact kept the apostles going.

Seven strands of testimony verify the resurrection of Jesus Christ. We have the evidence of the empty tomb; the evidence of the appearances recorded in the New Testament; the evidence of the dramatic change in the disciples from timid cowards to bold victors; the evidence of the Lord's day; the testimony of the saints over the centuries; the evidence of Jesus' inimitable achievements in history; and the evidence of our own personal experiences with the living Lord.

This evidence leads to only one logical conclusion: Jesus did indeed arise from the dead, and He is, therefore, the Son of God. That conclusion provides a place to stand for the Christian, a foundation which cannot be shaken.

Education (1:4-11)

The apostles needed more than a place to stand. They needed directions about which way to go and what to say. They needed more than evidence. They also needed education. Again, the resurrected Lord provided for their needs. Luke said Jesus spent forty days talking to the apostles (Acts 1:3). During this time, they began to work on their master's degree in discipleship. Jesus taught the apostles about three subjects.

1. The Kingdom of God (1:3,6-7)

Luke explained that Jesus spent the forty days "speaking of the things concerning the kingdom of God" (1:3). The resurrected Lord taught the apostles about the nature and scope of the kingdom of God. He taught that the kingdom of God was *not political but spiritual.* "My kingdom is not of this world," Jesus said (John 18:36, KJV). He taught that the kingdom of God was *not national but universal.* "For God so loved the world," Jesus proclaimed, "that He gave His only begotten Son, that whoever believes in Him should not perish, but have eternal life" (John 3:16). He taught that the kingdom of God was *not earned but received.* Jesus declared, "Truly I say to you, whoever does not receive the kingdom of God like a child shall not enter it at all" (Mark 10:15). He taught that the kingdom was *not temporal but eternal.* An angel said to Mary about Jesus, "The Lord God will give Him the throne of His father David; and He will reign over the house of Jacob forever; and His kingdom will have no end" (Luke 1:32-33). He taught that the kingdom of God was *not future but present.* "But if I cast out demons by the Spirit of God," Jesus affirmed, "then the kingdom of God has come upon you" (Matt. 12:28). He taught that the kingdom of God was *not secondary but primary.* "Seek first His kingdom and His righteousness; and all these things shall be added to you" (Matt. 6:33).

Jesus reaffirmed all these truths about the kingdom of God to the apostles. He gave them the information they needed to carry out their mission.

2. The Holy Spirit (1:4-5,8)

Jesus told the apostles to go to Jerusalem and wait "for what the Father had promised" (1:4). As Galileans, they would not have gone back to Jerusalem, especially in light of the recent events. The fact that they went back to Jerusalem indicates their obedience to Jesus. For what were they to wait? Jesus said they were to wait for the Holy Spirit. "Not many days from now" Jesus said, they would "be baptized with the Holy Spirit" (1:5).

This was not the origin of the Holy Spirit. The Holy Spirit was already active in the Old Testament period: in creation (Gen. 1:1-2), in prophecy (2 Pet. 1:20-21), and in the writing of Scripture (Heb. 10:15-16). The Holy Spirit was already active in the ministry of Jesus as Luke emphasized in his Gospel (1:35; 2:25; 3:16; 4:1; 10:21; and 12:12). Pentecost was not the beginning of the Holy Spirit's work. Nevertheless, Pentecost did mark something new about the Holy Spirit.

At Pentecost, *the Holy Spirit came to dwell in all believers.* In the Old Testament, the Spirit of God came just to special individuals, to prophets, priests, and kings, for special purposes. After Pentecost, the Holy Spirit was a gift to every believer. The first deacons were filled with the Spirit (Acts 6:3). Stephen was filled with the Spirit (Acts 6:3) as was Barnabas (Acts 11:22-24). Paul was filled with the Spirit (Acts 9:17). The Ephesian Christians were filled with the Spirit (Acts 20:28). The Holy Spirit was for all believers.

At Pentecost, *the Holy Spirit was given never to be withdrawn.* In the Old Testament, the Holy Spirit was given to individuals like Samson and Saul but later taken away from them (see Judg. 16:20-21 for Samson; 1 Sam. 16:14 for Saul). After Pentecost, Jesus promised His apostles: "I will ask the Father, and He will give you another Helper, that He may be with you forever" (John 14:16).

During those days in the graduate school of discipleship, Jesus taught the apostles about the Holy Spirit.

3. The Second Coming (1:6,9-11)

The resurrected Lord also taught the apostles about the second coming. When Jesus ascended to the Father, the apostles stood gazing into the heavens. Messengers from God gave them this assurance. Jesus Christ was coming again. Luke did not elaborate on what Jesus said about the second coming. Jesus refused to give a specific time for His return (Acts 1:7). To speculate on a precise time for Jesus' return is useless, because Jesus said that even He did not know the day and the hour (Mark 13:32). We don't know when Jesus will return. Two things, however, are clear:

Jesus will return personally. The angels said, "This Jesus, who has been taken up from you into heaven, will come in just the same way" (1:11).

A tourist was traveling along the shore of Lake Como in northern Italy. At the Villa Asconati, the friendly gardener opened the gate and showed him the grounds which the old man kept in perfect order. The tourist asked him when the owner of the castle had last been there. "Twelve years ago," the gardener answered.

The tourist replied, "But you keep this garden in such fine condition, just as though you expected your master to come tomorrow."

The gardener promptly replied, "Today, sir, today!" He knew his master would return personally.

Jesus will return triumphantly. When Jesus described His coming in Matthew 25:31, He said He would return "in His glory." How different the second coming will be from Jesus' first coming. Once He came in weakness, then He will come in power. Once He came in humility, then He will come in glory. Once He came in obscurity, then He will come in universal acclaim. He came the first time as a wandering rabbi of Palestine who was rejected by men and put to death on the cross. He will come the second time as the Lord of life, and before Him every knee shall bow, and every tongue confess that He is Lord!

Those were the lessons the apostles learned from the Master. That knowledge fortified them as they carried out their assignment.

Establishment (1:12-26)

The apostles also needed to be established on a firm foundation, emotionally and organizationally. That happened in verses 12-26.

Luke described the place where this coming together occurred as "the upper room" (Acts 1:13). Tradition affirms this "upper room," like the room where the last supper was held, to be the house of John Mark's mother, Mary. The apostles would meet there again in a time of crisis, when Peter was arrested, to pray for Peter's release (Acts 12:12).

Who participated in this gathering in the upper room? The band of apostles, minus Judas Iscariot, were all there (1:13). In addition, some of the women who had followed Jesus were there (1:14). Jesus' family was also there. These family members who had opposed Jesus during His ministry (John 7:5) were now among His supporters. These who had been His family in the flesh were now a part of His spiritual family. With such a motley group, Jesus would literally turn the world upside down! This is a clear demonstration of that truth written into all of history: Little is much when God is in it.

In an Eastern European country a young woman heard the gospel and was converted. Her communist parents made her leave home. In the course of six months, her quiet but effective witness resulted in the conversion of seven students at the school she attended. Consequently, she was expelled. She obtained a job in a bakery, and within the next six months she won ten of her fellow workers to faith in Christ. She lost her job and citizenship. She was exiled. But in another country she was instrumental in the formation of a church with forty members! Little is much when God is in it.

These first Christian leaders gathered in the upper room had a problem. Judas's betrayal led eventually to his self-inflicted death (1:18). On the basis of Psalm 69:25 and Psalm 109:8, the apostles believed Judas's position needed to be filled. What qualifications were demanded for this new apostle? He had to have been with Jesus since His baptism (1:21). He had to be a witness to the resurrection (1:22). He had to receive the appointment of Christ Himself (1:24).

After carefully considering the options, the apostles discovered two men who were qualified. They used a time-honored method of discerning the will of God: casting lots. The names of the individuals were written on stones. The stones were put into a container. Then, the container was shaken until one of the stones feel out. The stone which came out had on it the name of Matthias.

Remember two things about this process. First, the apostles were convinced that Jesus Himself was in control of the process. They combined their casting of lots with this prayer: "Thou, Lord, who knowest the hearts of all men, show which one of these two Thou hast chosen" (1:24). The Old Testament confirmed the same truth: "The lot is cast into the lap; but the whole disposing thereof is of the Lord" (Prov. 16:33, KJV). This was not a haphazard process of human will. It was a method for determining God's will.

Second, this is the last time this method of discerning truth is referred to in the Bible. From that point on, Christians would have the Holy Spirit within them. This Holy Spirit, according to the promise of Jesus, would guide them into all the truth (John 16:13).

Simply organizing the group with the selection of a new apostle, however, was not enough to establish these first Christians and prepare them for what was ahead. They needed a unity of spirit and an anticipation of what God had in store for them. How would these first Christians be molded into one? How would they be established? We see the answer in Acts 1:14. Luke told us, "These all with one mind were continually devoting themselves to prayer."

How can we today experience that oneness which will fortify us as we move out to do God's work? How can we come together as God's people? The answer is the same as it was in the first century: prayer. Prayer is the thermostat that determines the spiritual temperature of any Christian or any church. Paul Powell says that we must meet God in a holy place before we can minister effectively for Him in the marketplace.[1] Prayer will unite us as God's people and give us a foundation from which we can launch out into the world. That's what the first Christians did. They met with God in the holy place of the upper room. With one mind they united their hearts in prayer.

Empowerment (2:1-13)

The apostles needed one more ingredient. They needed empowerment. That empowerment came with the Holy Spirit in Acts 2. The popularity of this second chapter of Acts is beyond question. G. Campbell Morgan said, "Perhaps there is no chapter in the New Testament which has been read more often than this."[2] Acts 2 is one of the best known and best loved parts of God's Word because it describes the power by which the church carries out its ministry.

1. The Setting (2:1)

Notice the setting of this remarkable event. Luke began, "And when the day of Pentecost had come" (2:1). Pentecost, which occurred fifty days after the Passover, was one of the three great feasts that every male Israelite was expected to attend in Jerusalem (the Feast of Tabernacles and Passover were the other two). Every year, the city was swelled with the population of the pilgrims who came to Jerusalem to be a part of this great feast. This was a time of expectancy and sensitivity.

2. The Sound (2:2)

As the apostles gathered in the upper room, they heard a sound. Luke said, "Suddenly, there came from heaven a noise like a violent, rushing wind" (2:2). In the Scriptures, the wind often symbolized the presence of God. We see this in Ezekiel's vision of dry bones (Ezek. 37:9-14). The wind, representing the presence of God, breathed life into the dry bones, set them on their feet, and made them come alive. The wind symbolized the presence of God. We see the same connection in Jesus' discussion with Nicodemus in John 3. Jesus used a play on words between *wind* and *Spirit* to communicate to Nicodemus the mystery of God's presence in human life.

The sound of a mighty, rushing wind that filled the room declared to all who heard it, "God is here. God is at work."

3. The Sight (2:3)

These apostles not only heard something but also saw something. Luke declared, "There appeared to them tongues as of fire distributing themselves, and they rested on each of them" (2:3). Like wind, fire was a symbol of the presence of God. In Moses' encounter with God in the wilderness, he saw a bush aglow with fire which was not consumed by the fire (Ex. 3). The fire represented the presence of God.

The tongues of fire perhaps had another meaning. Among the Jews of that day, it was a commonly held belief that an appearance like fire often encircled the heads of distinguished teachers of the law. When the tongues of fire rested on each of the heads of the Christians gathered in the upper room, this symbolized that they had been empowered by the Spirit of God to be communicators. God was saying, "Listen to what these men say, for they speak the truth."

4. The Speech (2:4-13)

We see yet another peculiar phenomenon of that Pentecostal event, the speech of the apostles. The Bible says, "They were all filled with the Holy Spirit and began to speak with other tongues, as the Spirit was giving them utterance" (2:4). This is the most difficult and most controversial part of the passage. The experience of *glossolalia* (speaking in tongues) is one of the most prominent religious phenomena of our day. However, the Bible itself says little about glossolalia. In the Book of Acts, which tells the story of the experience of the early church, the phenomenon of tongues is referred to only three times—in our text, in Acts 10, and in Acts 19. Noticeable differences distinguish these three experiences.

The tongues in Acts 10 and 19 were evidently utterances in unknown tongues and were an outward sign that the conversion of the Gentiles and the conversion of the disciples of John were valid works of God. Tongues, in these instances, had sign value as evidence of the work of God.

The tongues in Acts 2, on the other hand, were known tongues.
Jews from all over the world were in Jerusalem for the Pentecost celebration, many who spoke only the dialects and languages native to
their land. Therefore, on the day of Pentecost, God gave the apostles
the special ability to speak, not in unknown tongues, but in the
tongues and dialects of the people who were there, so that everyone
could hear and understand their message. Those listening said, "We
hear them in our own tongues speaking of the mighty deeds of God"
(2:11). Tongues, in this instance, had value as a tool to communicate
the good news of Christ.

Not the manner of the apostles' speech but the content of their
speech was most important at Pentecost. The real miracle was not the
tongues but the power of God which transformed those apostles into
bold emissaries of a resurrected Christ and enabled them to effectively communicate the gospel. That is the dimension of the Pentecostal
event we should seek to emulate today. We should be men and
women who, under the power of God's Spirit, boldly communicate
His good news to the world.

5. The Spirit (2:4)

In looking at the amazing account in Acts, we have noted the set
ting, the sound, the sight, and the speech. We cannot close this section without looking at the central element of the entire experience:
the Spirit. The most important factor about the Pentecostal experi
ence was not that it happened on the day of Pentecost; was not that
the sound of a mighty, rushing wind filled the room; was not that
tongues of fire rested on each head; and was not that the apostles
were able to speak in other languages and dialects. The central feature of the experience was that the Spirit of God came upon the apostles in a new, dynamic way. The event at Pentecost marks the coming
of the Spirit in power to the church. Luke used two words in reference to the spirit: baptized (1:5) and filled (2:4).

What does it mean to be "baptized with the Holy Spirit?" The baptism of the Spirit is the act of God by which He identifies the believer

as a part of the family of God (1 Cor. 12:13). The baptism of the Spirit that happened historically at Pentecost happens individually when ever a person is born into the family of God.

What does it mean to be "filled with the Holy Spirit?" The filling of the Spirit happens every time we open ourselves more to the control and purpose of God (Eph. 5:18).

Warren Wiersbe has correctly stated: "The baptism of the Spirit means that I belong to His body; the fullness of the Spirit means that my body belongs to Him. The baptism is final; the fullness is repeated as we trust God for new power to witness."[3]

How ineffective the church often appears today. How weak we are in our attempt to carry out the work of God. Like the early Christians, we need a fresh experience with the Holy Spirit.

When John Hyde boarded the ship to go from England to India for his first missionary tour, he was handed a telegram. He opened it hurriedly on the deck of the ship. The only words in the telegram were, "John Hyde, are you filled with the Spirit of God?" The note aroused Hyde's anger. He crumpled the paper, put it into his pocket, and went to bed.

Unable to sleep, he tossed and turned all night. He arose from bed in the early morning hours, took the piece of paper out of his pocket, and read it again. He thought, *The audacity of somebody to ask me that question, "Am I filled with the Holy Spirit?" Here I am a missionary, sincere, dedicated, leaving my home and going to another country. How dare someone ask me if I am filled with the Spirit.*

Suddenly, Hyde's spirit was touched by the challenge of the note, and he fell to his knees before the Father. "O God," he cried out, "the audacity of me to think that I could pray or preach or witness or live or serve or do anything in my own strength and power. Fill me with Your strength. Fill me with Your power." John Hyde became one of the great missionary statesmen of all time. Why? Because of the power of the Spirit which enabled him to face the challenges of his life in the power of God.

That is what happened to these first apostles. When the Holy Spirit indwelled them as a permanent gift to empower them, they were at last ready to move out into the world and carry out the assignment given to them. We'll monitor their progress as witnesses for Christ in the next chapter.

2 Witnesses for Christ

Acts 2:14-47

Over lunch with four young leaders in our church, I asked the question, "What business are we in right now as a church?" One suggested the primary business of the church is to teach. Another of these young leaders said our main business as a church is to provide Christian fellowship. The third young man made his suggestion. He thought the church's primary role is to support and encourage Christians, another manifestation of fellowship. The fourth young man agreed with the others.

How would you answer the question: What is the main business of the church? The New Testament suggests our main business is reaching people. Teaching, fellowship, and encouragement are effective methods in carrying out that responsibility. Our primary challenge, however, is to reach people. The word we use to describe this task is *evangelism.*

After laying the foundation, the apostles were ready to carry out the task Jesus had given them to do. They were ready to evangelize. Luke described the message and method of New Testament evangelism.

The Proclamation (2:14-36)

At no point do we see such a contrast between the church of the first century and the church of today as in our preaching. When these first Christians preached, God's power was felt, and lives were changed. When we preach today, so often we do not experience this power and change. Many factors can be cited for this difference.

Sometimes, it is a lack of preparation. A pastor entered the pulpit one morning with a huge Band-Aid on his chin. He explained that, while shaving, he had his mind on his sermon and had cut his chin. Someone suggested he should have kept his mind on his shaving and cut his sermon!

Sometimes, it is a lack of enthusiasm. A pastor had an actor friend who was drawing large crowds at his performances, while the pastor was preaching to only a few in the church. The preacher asked his actor friend, "Why do you draw great crowds, and I have no audience at all? Your words are sheer fiction, and mine are unchangeable truths."

The actor answered, "I present my fiction as though it were truth; you present your truth as though it were fiction."

Sometimes, it is a lack of communication. A pastor was told by a young man one morning that he must be smarter than Einstein. The pastor asked him what he meant. The young man said, "Einstein was so smart that only ten men in the world could understand him. But I don't believe anybody can understand you!"

The basic failure in today's pulpit is not a lack of preparation, not a lack of enthusiasm, nor a lack of communication. Our basic problem is a failure to proclaim the New Testament message. Paul told the Galatian Christians he was amazed they had so soon turned to another gospel, which was not really a gospel at all (1:6-7). The gospel, however, has not changed. It is the same gospel that rocked the Roman world on its ear, the same gospel that sent Paul streaking across Asia Minor, the same gospel that sparked the Reformation, the same gospel that sent David Livingston to Africa, and the same gospel that is proclaimed by Billy Graham to millions today. In this first recorded sermon of the early church, which is one of the ten sermons recorded in the New Testament, we see the basic ingredients of the gospel.

1. A Message About God (2:22)

Peter began with this affirmation: "Men of Israel, listen to these words: Jesus the Nazarene, a man attested to you by God with miracles and wonders and signs which God performed through Him in your midst" (2:22). These first-century Christians preached about God and what He had done in history.

The gospel is not primarily a new ethic, nor is it simply a call to brotherliness. Neither is it a new philosophy of life nor a new social program for righting the wrongs of our social order. In the end, the gospel included these things. It presented a new ethic, created a new quality of brotherliness, supplied a new philosophy, and enunciated a new program for society. However, the gospel is a message about God. The gospel is the proclamation that the living God who has existed throughout all eternity has at one definite point and in one definite Person broken into history. Once and for all, in that one particular life—the life of Jesus—God has given us the full and final revelation of Himself. The eternal God became flesh and dwelt among us (John 1:14).

2. A Message About the Cross (2:23)

What did this God do when He broke into history? Peter said, "This Man, delivered up by the predetermined plan and foreknowledge of God, you nailed to a cross by the hands of godless men and put Him to death" (2:23). In the middle of history, God set a cross; and from that day until this, the heart of the Christian message, the identifying mark of the Christian church, and the exhilarating guarantee of a new life is the cross. What does the cross mean for us?

The cross is an *illustration of human sin.* The cross shatters our rationalizations about sin and reminds us that sin is not just ignorance that can be corrected by education. Sin is not a maladjustment that can be corrected by developing new relationships. Sin is not a moral lapse that can easily be rectified by turning over a new leaf. Sin is something so tragic, so devastating, that it takes the shed blood of a perfect Savior to rectify it. The cross is an illustration of the sinfulness of sin.

The cross is *a revelation of God's love.* In the same event in which sin was unveiled in its vilest depths, the love of God was also revealed in its loftiest heights. The cross was not just the act of men, as if by some act of fate Christ's life was accidently crushed by the turning wheel of history. Peter said the cross happened according to God's prearranged plan (2:23). We have not said the final word about the cross until we say that the cross was the very act of God by which He revealed in history's most sublime way His incredible love for humankind.

The cross is *an invitation to life.* To millions down through the centuries, the cross has been more than an illustration of the horror of sin or a revelation of the love of God. It has been an invitation to new life. Gipsy Smith, an evangelist of another age, said, "I am not afraid of the cross. I know that men used to come there to die, but since He died, they come there to live."[1]

The cross was a stumbling block to the Jews, a scandal to the Greeks, and a mystery to many modern day skeptics. But to those who believe, both Jew and Greek, it has been the power of God unto salvation (1 Cor. 1:23-24). These early proclaimers of the Word preached about the cross.

3. A Message About the Resurrection (2:24,32)

The death of Jesus was answered by His resurrection. Peter declared, "God raised Him up again, putting an end to the agony of death, since it was impossible for Him to be held in its power" (2:24). He added, "This Jesus God raised up again, to which we are all witnesses" (2:32). Like Simon Peter, the other early proclaimers of the Word never pointed people to the cross without showing them the resurrection light breaking behind it. The resurrection of Jesus Christ is not a postscript to the gospel, an appendix to the faith which we can take or leave at our own whim. It is the faith. Jesus Christ did not stay in the grave, but He is arisen, and He lives today. By their words, their walk, and their words, the first Christians declared the resurrection. What does the resurrection mean?

The resurrection is *a pronouncement of victory.* The resurrection was not just the survival of one individual from the grave. It was the herald of God's victory over death for all persons. This was the thunderbolt that electrified the apostles. This is the certainty that burns undimmed in every Christian heart today. The power that raised Jesus will someday resurrect the world and, bringing captivity captive, will usher in the kingdom of God in all its fullness.

The resurrection is also *a promise of a living presence.* The statement Jesus made to His disciples in the Great Commission was no empty promise or rhetorical pulpit pronouncement, but the deepest experience of every Christian through the centuries: "I am with you always, even to the end of the age" (Matt. 28:20). Jesus Christ died but is alive again, and He is alive today. May we never cease to preach the thrilling message of the resurrected Lord.

4. A Message About Life (2:33)

God has acted in history through the cross and resurrection of Jesus Christ to open for humankind the way to new life. To the question of the rich young ruler, "What shall I do to inherit eternal life?" (Mark 10:17), these first-century preachers had only one answer, "There is salvation in no one else; for there is no other name under heaven that has been given among men, by which we must be saved" (Acts 4:12).

Jesus Himself confirmed this truth when He said, "I am the way, and the truth, and the life: no one comes to the Father, but through Me" (John 14:6). Peter declared in his Pentecost sermon that the resurrected Christ "has poured forth this which you both see and hear" (2:33).

This message broke through the darkness of the first-century world like a streak of lightning as men and women dazed by sin, disillusioned by life, and discouraged by the seeming meaninglessness of existence were told that there was a way in which they could have their sins forgiven, their lives given new direction, and their existence given new meaning. That way to life was Jesus Christ.

The gospel we must proclaim, the message we must use to evangelize the world, is this same message about God, about the cross, about the resurrection, and about life!

The Pattern (2:37-41)

Following the proclamation of the gospel message, Peter pressed for a response. What was the pattern of this response?

1. Conviction (2:37)

When the gospel was proclaimed, the listeners "were pierced to the heart" (v. 37). According to Jesus, it is the Holy Spirit who carries out this convicting work, not the evangelist. Jesus said about the Holy Spirit, "And He, when He comes, will convict [*elegchei*] the world concerning sin, and righteousness, and judgment" (John 16:8). The Greek word *elegchei* appears in the New Testament seventeen times and is translated eight different ways. Two basic ideas are involved.

First, the word means *to convict.* Convict is a judicial term with forensic meanings. This word finds its setting in the courtroom. A person is on trial. The evidence is presented. The jury withdraws to the jury room and later returns. The foreman of the jury hands the decision to the judge, and he announces, "The jury has found the defendant guilty." That's conviction.

Second, the word can also mean *to convince.* Convince is a persuasive term which has to do not with the facts but with our acceptance of those facts. The person in the courtroom hears the verdict of the jury, "Guilty." Something inside of him responds to that conviction with positive acceptance. "They are right," the man says to himself. "I am guilty." That's convincing.

When the gospel is preached, the Holy Spirit awakens in the heart of the listener a sense of guilt and brings her to the point where she is ready to admit it.

2. Confession (2:38-40)

Conviction must lead to confession. The gospel demands a decision from the listener. To the question, "What shall we do?" Peter answered, "Repent, and let each of you be baptized in the name of Jesus Christ" (v. 38). It is one thing to agree that we are sinners. It is another thing to be willing to give up our sins. It is one thing to acknowledge we are going in the wrong direction. It is another thing to turn from that way and begin to go in the right direction. Repentance involves a change of attitude toward our sins which in turn leads to a change of action.

A young boy was scoldingly asked by his mother, "Aren't you ashamed staying in bed past noon every day?"

The boy answered, "Yes, I am ashamed, but I would rather be ashamed than to get up!" Being ashamed of our sin is not enough. Being convicted about our sin is not enough. Conviction must lead to confession.

3. Conversion (2:41)

Confession then will lead to conversion. Luke said, "So then, those who had received his word were baptized" (v. 41). When the gospel is received, it brings about a change of life.

Edward Studd of England made a fortune in North India in the nineteenth century. Because he lost a bet to a friend, the friend made Studd attend a revival service in which Dwight L. Moody preached. Studd sat on the first row and never took his eyes off Moody. He returned the next night and then each successive night until he was converted. Studd lived only two years after that time, but it was said at his funeral that he accomplished more for Christ in two years than most did in twenty years. Studd turned his mansion into a meeting place for Christians. He wrote his friends and told them they needed to turn to Christ. He called on his tailor and shirtmaker and spoke of Christ. His coachman gave this assessment of Edward Studd: "All I can say is that though there's the same skin, there's a new man inside."[2] When the gospel message is preached, lives are changed by the power of God.

The Product (2:42-47)

Nine times in the Book of Acts, Luke paused to give a summary statement of the status of the church. In this first summary, Luke pictured the product of evangelism. The ultimate aim of evangelism is not only to produce converts but also to produce disciples. Converts become disciples when they are involved in the kind of church Luke described in these verses.

1. A Learning Church (2:42)

Luke said about these first Christians, "They were continually devoting themselves to the apostles' teaching" (v. 42). Too many Christians and too many churches are "fixated children of God." That is, once they are saved, they think they are through. They have fixated their understanding of God at a child's level and have not grown in their understanding since that time. They have quit growing because they have quit studying.

The Word of God contains an inexhaustible supply of spiritual truths that we cannot completely comprehend in a dozen lifetimes. As a seminary professor used to tell his students, "To study infinity requires eternity." Therefore, the study of God's Word must be a lifetime commitment.

Converts become disciples through the continued study of God's Word.

2. A Fellowshiping Church (2:42,44-45)

These first Christians not only devoted themselves to the apostle's teachings but also "to fellowship" (v. 42). The Greek word *koinonia* means fellowship, but it means more than that. It declares our oneness in Christ Jesus.

A little boy was asked to define fellowship. He said, "I guess it is two fellows in a ship." That's not a bad definition because when two fellows are in a ship together, they go up and down together, move forward at the same pace, and they are together in a common purpose. That's what fellowship is.

Converts become disciples through fellowship with other Christians in the church.

3. A Praying Church (2:42)

These first Christians also devoted themselves "to prayer" (v. 42). These early Christians discovered they could not get through life in their own strength. Then they made an even more remarkable discovery. They did not have to face life in their own strength. They could face life in God's strength which came to them through prayer.

William Barclay expressed it this way: "They always spoke to God before they spoke with man; they always went into God before they went out to the world; they could meet the problems of life because they had first met God."[3]

Converts are transformed into disciples through the practice of prayer.

4. A Reverent Church (2:43)

Luke said, "Everyone kept feeling a sense of awe" (v. 43). An essential ingredient in every church is a sense of reverential fear and awe which causes us to acknowledge that all we have comes from God. Do not equate reverence with formality. By fear and reverence, I do not mean formality, nor do I mean that there should be no enthusiastic expression of our emotions.

One young man came into a formal congregation and sat on the front row. He was enthusiastic and expressive. After the first hymn, he said, "Amen." Then following the solo, he shouted, "Praise the Lord!" When the preacher made his opening remark, the young man declared, "Preach on."

Finally, one of the members who could stand it no more said to the visitor, "Sir, you are going to have to be quiet."

"But you don't understand," said the visitor, "I've got religion."

"Well," responded the member, "you didn't get it here!"

Reverence is not an outward manifestation but an inner conviction. On the one hand, you can be very formal and solemn and dignified in your worship. On the other hand, you can punctuate the service with "Praise the Lords" and cry huge tears every time the choir sings "The King Is Coming." You can be reverent or irreverent in either case. Reverence is not an outward manifestation but an inner conviction that all we are comes from God and is dependent on Him, that this is God's church we are a part of, and that this is God's work we are about.

Converts are developed into disciples in the context of reverence.

5. An Achieving Church (2:43)

Luke's statement in verse 43, "Many wonders and signs were taking place through the apostles," indicates that exciting achievements were happening in the Jerusalem church.

Someone has distinguished three groups in the church: the plus-plus group, the plus-minus groups, and the minus-minus group. The plus-plus group says, "I can do it, you can do it, so let's get it done." The plus-minus crowd says, "I can do it, you can't do it, so get out of my way." The minus-minus crowd says, "I can't do it, you can't do it either, and whoever brought it up in the first place?"

Converts become disciples in churches which expect great things from God and thus achieve great things for God.

6. A Happy Church (2:46)

Luke told us these first Christians "were taking their meals together with gladness and with sincerity of heart, praising God" (v. 46).

Many Christians are like the woman at the football game. She was freezing. Someone had spilled his drink on her. She was sick on the popcorn she ate. Her team was behind forty to nothing. Shivering, she turned to her husband and said, "Honey, tell me again how much fun we're having." Jesus came so that His joy might be in us, and so that our joy might be full. A church that isn't happy, doesn't have fun, and never laughs is not the church of Jesus Christ.

Converts are made into disciples in the context of a joy-filled church.

7. An Attractive Church (2:47)

The Jerusalem church was an attractive church. As they worshiped daily in the temple and took their food with gladness, these early Christians were "having favor with all the people" (v. 47).

When a church caught on fire, two church members stood watching. One turned to the other and said, "This is the first time I have seen you at church in ten years."

The other responded, "This is the first time this church has been on fire!" When the members of a church are excited about the work of the Lord, when they are genuinely and sincerely committed to God's work, and when a church is on fire, people are going to come to watch it burn. People are hungry for something to give meaning to their lives. When they see that possibility in the church, they will come. In that kind of church, converts are transformed into disciples.

Evangelism is the main business of the church. However, evangelism involves more than winning converts. Evangelism also involves enlisting these new Christians in the church so they can be mobilized to carry out God's work.

3 | The Church at Work

Acts 3:1—4:37

Thomas Aquinas called on Pope Innocent in the thirteenth century. The Pope, who was counting a large sum of money that had come to the church, told Aquinas, "See, Thomas, the church can no longer say, 'Silver and gold have I none.' "

"True, holy father," Aquinas responded, "but neither can she now say, 'Arise and walk.' "[1]

Obviously, the church of the twentieth century can no longer say, "Silver and gold have I none." Many churches have budgets in excess of one million dollars. No longer can we say, "Silver and gold have I none." The disturbing question is whether or not we can still say to broken humanity around us, "Arise and walk." We have the provisions, but do we still have the power? We have the coins, but do we still have the compassion? We are gathering together in increasing numbers to be a part of the worship of the church. Are we with equal concern and intensity involving ourselves in the work of the church?

The evangelistic witness of the apostles resulted in additions to the church. Now it was time for these new Christians to begin doing the work of the church.

Working for Jesus (3:1-10)

Luke said, "Many wonders and signs were taking place through the apostles" (Acts 2:43). He singled out one of these "wonders and signs" for special attention, one that had received considerable publicity.

1. The Problem (3:1-4)

The story begins: "Peter and John were going up to the Temple at the ninth hour, the hour of prayer" (3:1). Although the Jews believed prayer to be effective wherever it was offered, they felt it was more effective if offered in the temple. Three times a day, a pious Jew would go to the temple to pray. We see the apostles continuing this custom.

As Peter and John approached the temple they saw a man "who had been lame from his mother's womb" (3:2). The man was more than forty years of age (4:22). This man had a problem, a serious condition that had been with him all of his life. This was no fraudulent attempt to persuade the people of the power of Peter. It was a real problem of which all the people were aware. The man's friends set him by the entrance to the temple each day, not to be healed, but so that he could beg alms from the people who would probably be more generous as they went into the temple to worship God. This man with the serious problem fixed his attention on Peter and John "expecting to receive something from them" (3:5). In today's church, we are also surrounded by people who have serious problems, many which have been with them for a long time, and they have fixed their attention on the church expecting to receive something from us.

Some people have *economic problems.* More than twenty-six million Americans are below the poverty level. Most who have sufficient money are not using it wisely. One sociologist estimated that one of every three young families in America today are only one paycheck away from bankruptcy. A plastic surgeon said the most successful operation he ever performed was when he cut up his credit cards!

People also have *emotional problems.* A noted psychiatrist from the University of Louisville claims we are entering an era of depression, an ailment 20 percent of the United States population suffers from at the present time. With the growing emotional upheaval of our day, it is not surprising to hear that every eighty-six seconds someone in our world commits suicide. That is at the clip of about 1,000 persons a day.

People also have *interpersonal problems.* The emotional problems, in part, come from a lack of significant others in our lives with whom we can share and from whom we can gain support. The most serious interpersonal problem of our time is loneliness. Loneliness haunts senior adults, troubles young people, and plagues most of us in between.

Some suffer from *intellectual problems.* More than twenty million Americans cannot read or write; that is one out of every five adults. About 40 percent of the world's population cannot read and write. Lack of knowledge is a serious problem for many today.

People of our day are also haunted by *family problems.* In the United States, marriages are splitting at the rate of about one million every year. The resulting problems between parents and children and the pressures with which we are confronted make us wonder what happened to the song "There's no place like home."

In addition, there are also *physical problems.* More than ten million people will starve to death this year. Our hospitals are full, and our health care industry is being pushed to its limits. In many cases, we are contributing directly to our problems. A cartoon showed an older gentleman reading a paper in which the headlines cited high cholesterol levels and potential carcinogens found in various foods. The man said to his wife, "Everything you eat, drink, breathe, or do these days is a health risk! You're only safe just sitting in your living room doing nothing!"

At that moment, the radio blared out, "This just in. Researchers announced today that tests conducted on laboratory rats confirm that just sitting in a living room doing nothing can cause lower back pain, fallen arches . . ."

Two boys were fighting on the school ground. One of the other children ran for help. He said to the teacher, "Teacher, teacher, two boys are fighting, and the one on the bottom would like to see you." The ones on the bottom in the struggle of life, like the man in the story in Acts 3, have fixed their attention on those of us who call ourselves the church, and they are waiting to see what we will do. The hurting of the world are crying out for our help.

2. The Philosophy (3:5-6)

How did Peter respond to this hurt? Peter said, "I do not possess silver and gold, but what I do have I give to you . . ." (3:6). Confronted by the cries of a needy world, this is the philosophy which the church adopted: "Such as I have, I give."

Remember the scene. Peter and John were on their way to worship. They were pulled by their passion to pray. Prayer is certainly a worthy undertaking. Yet, the apostles did not let their compulsion to worship keep them from stopping and ministering to the man in need.

As a jury returned to the courtroom to announce their verdict, the chairman of the jury announced: "We have voted not to get involved!" Ridiculous, isn't it? No more ridiculous is the stance of that jury than for the church to stand in the midst of this world of pain and problems polishing our halos while the world self-destructs.

"Voluntary sacrifice, in the will of God, motivated by love, to care for the total needs of men." That's the way Bill Pinson has expressed it in our day.[2] "What I do have I give." That's the way Simon Peter expressed it in our text. Either way you say it, the philosophy is the same: We are to use the resources of the church to minister to the needs of people in the name of Christ.

3. The Product (3:7-10)

In verses 7-10, Luke described the product of this caring philosophy of the church. When Peter took the lame man's hand, he stood on his feet. The man felt strength rushing through his feet, so he ran through the temple demonstrating his healing. Here's the equation: human need $+$ Christian compassion $+$ God's power $=$ miraculous change in human life.

Preaching About Jesus (3:11—4:4)

The work of the church was not only to help those with problems but also to herald the message of the gospel. When the healed man ran through the temple, leaping and praising God, a crowd gathered

(3:8). Peter preached to the crowd.

1. The Contact (3:11-13)

The New Testament preachers recognized the importance of starting where the people were in their preaching. When Paul preached to the Athenians, he began with the altar to the unknown God (Acts 17:23). When Philip preached to the Ethiopian, he began with the Scripture of Isaiah where the Ethiopian was reading (Acts 8:35). In this instance, when Peter preached to the Jews, he began by referring to "The God of Abraham, Isaac, and Jacob, the God of our fathers" (v. 13).

The church is responsible for bringing the gospel message in contact with human lives. When we shoot over our listener's heads, it does not mean we have superior ammunition. It simply means we don't know how to shoot!

2. The Content (3:13—4:4)

Each of the sermons of the New Testament is different because the preachers were different and because the circumstances in which they preached were different. Nevertheless, each of the New Testament messages focused on Jesus, and each followed a common outline that included four points.

First, the preachers alluded to the Old Testament Scriptures fulfilled in the life and ministry of Jesus. Peter said about Jesus, "But the things which God announced beforehand by the mouth of all the prophets, that His Christ should suffer, He has thus fulfilled" (3:18).

Second, the preachers analyzed Jesus' ministry. Always, they included Jesus' death and resurrection. Peter said about the life and ministry of Jesus: "The one whom you delivered up, and disowned in the presence of Pilate, when he had decided to release Him. But you disowned the Holy and Righteous One, and asked for a murderer to be granted to you, but put to death the Prince of life" (3:13-15). Peter said about the resurrection of Jesus: "The one whom God raised from the dead, a fact to which we are witnesses" (3:15).

Third, the preachers made an announcement about who Jesus was.

Peter called Jesus "the Christ appointed for you" (3:20). In the Pentecost sermon, Peter declared, "God has made Him both Lord and Christ—this Jesus whom you crucified" (Acts 2:36).

Finally, the preachers made an appeal. After outlining briefly who Jesus was, Peter said, "Repent therefore and return, that your sins may be wiped away" (3:19). The ultimate aim of New Testament preaching was to lead people to repentance.

What is *repentance?* The word literally means to think again or to turn. Repentance is not a permanent state of a person's life. Rather, it is a transition from one state to another. Thus understood, repentance has two dimensions.

Repentance has *a negative dimension. Repentance* means to turn from something. This aspect of repentance has to do with the past and presupposes the realization of an abnormal state of affairs in the past. Repentance begins when a person looks at the past and recognizes he or she is on the wrong road, acknowledges the mistake, and decides to turn from it.

Repentance also has *a positive dimension. Repentance* means to turn to something. This aspect of repentance has to do with the future and opens up to the repentant sinner a new way of life. To repent means that, after recognizing our mistakes and the dangers of our past situations, by a redirection of our whole beings, we enter into a new and right path of living in the future. Repentance is not only a mourner's bench where we walk the painful pathway of introspection that leads to confession. Repentance is also the launching pad where the soul is sent into a new eternal orbit with God at the center of the arc.

What happens when we repent? Peter suggested three results.

Repentance brings *forgiveness.* Peter said, "Repent . . . that your sins may be wiped away" (3:19). The words *wiped away* mean to rub off, to erase, and to wipe out. Picture all of our sins written on a chalk board. When we repent, Jesus erases all our sins off the board. He gives us a clean slate.

Repentance brings *refreshment.* Peter said, "Repent therefore and return, . . . in order that times of refreshing may come" (v. 19). When we repent, our relationship with God is renewed, resulting in a refreshing of our souls. David longed for this refreshing when he prayed, "Restore to me the joy of Thy salvation" (Ps. 51:12).

Repentance brings *hope*. Peter said, "Repent therefore and return, . . . that He may send Jesus, the Christ appointed for you" (vv. 19-20). The coming Peter had in mind was Jesus' second coming. When we repent, we are getting the world ready for the coming of our King. No wonder these first Christians called their message "good news." It is good news: good news of forgiveness, good news of refreshment, and good news of hope.

When the gospel is proclaimed, two contrasting responses are evident. Some reacted to the messengers and rejected the message (4:1-3). Others were convinced by the messengers and received the message (4:4). We should not be shocked by those who receive the message, nor should we be discouraged by those who do not. Instead, we should continue to faithfully proclaim the message.

Walking with Jesus (4:5-31)

In this fourth chapter of Acts we see the vitality and the vivaciousness of the apostles. How different from the picture painted in the Gospels. In Luke 22:57, we see Peter in cowardice, denying his Lord before the accusation of a servant girl, even shouting an oath that he did not know Jesus. In John 20:19, we see the disciples crouched in the seclusion of a room with the windows closed and the door bolted for fear of the Jews. In Luke 24:17, we see two of the followers of Jesus walking dejectedly down the Emmaus road, sad of countenance, disappointed because this Jesus whom they thought was to be their Messiah had been put to death.

Notice the difference after the resurrection. In the preresurrection days, the apostles were defeated. However, in Acts 4 they are victorious. Then they were fearful; now they are fearless. Then they were timid; now they are bold. Then they were weak; now they are powerful. The reason for the difference in these two pictures was a fact so obvious that even the leaders of the accusing council noticed it. The council which examined the apostles was the Sanhedrin—the supreme court of the Jews. As the leaders of the Sanhedrin examined the apostles they were amazed. When they saw the power of these two uneducated men, they recognized that they had been with Jesus (4:13).

What happened to these apostles when they walked with Jesus? What did they receive?

1. A New Personal Evaluation (4:5-13)

Peter and John were "uneducated and untrained men" (v. 13). They had no technical education and no professional qualifications. They lacked the scholastic privileges and the societal pedigree that according to the standards of the day would have made them important. They were nobodies, and they were standing before seventy-one of the most important men of that day. Annas, the high priest emeritus, was there. Caiaphas, the ruling high priest, was there. John and Alexander and all who were of high priestly descent were there. The Sadducees were there. The Pharisees were there. The elders, respected men in the community, were there.

Think of it! Two uneducated, untrained fishermen standing before a gathering of the most important men of that day. Remember also that this same Sanhedrin had only recently condemned Jesus to death. Yet, they stood before the members of the Sanhedrin with confidence, debated them convincingly, and amazed them with their power.

How did the apostles accomplish such a momentous feat? Their confidence came in the new personal evaluation given to them by Jesus. When they walked with Jesus, they realized their importance was not determined by who they were but by whose they were. They were important to God. They were valuable according to God's standards. That new personal evaluation gave them confidence and power.

2. A New Perspective (4:14-20)

When the Sanhedrin ordered the apostles to stop preaching about Jesus, Peter and John answered, "Whether it is right in the sight of

God to give heed to you rather than to God, you be the judge; for we cannot stop speaking what we have seen and heard" (vv. 19-20). Walking with Jesus convinced the first Christians that nothing was more important than pleasing God. Therefore, when they had to chose between pleasing God and pleasing people, they chose to please God.

A country preacher once said, "If you please God, it doesn't matter who you displease. If you displease God, it doesn't matter who you please." That was the perspective of the apostles, a perspective they received from having walked with Jesus.

On one occasion, Martin Luther was threatened by a representative of the Pope. The messenger reminded Luther of the papal power and warned him of a day when he would be deserted by his supporters. "Where will you be then?" Luther was asked.

He responded, "Then, as now, in the hands of almighty God!"[3]

3. A New Purpose (4:20-22)

The Sanhedrin ordered the apostles "not to speak or teach at all in the name of Jesus" (v. 18). The words of the Sanhedrin were unheeded. As W. Graham Scroggie expressed it, "The Council might as well have told the sun not to shine, and the tides not to move, and the winds not to blow, as to tell these men not to talk about Jesus."[4] Talking about Jesus was their very purpose for living!

The Bible suggests this as the motivating purpose in the life of every Christian. If you are a salesman, you will not only sell your product but you will also sell Jesus Christ. If you are a lawyer, you will find ways to tell people about their Heavenly Advocate who pleads their case before God. If you are a doctor, you will tell your patients about the Great Physician who can heal their souls. If you are a carpenter, you will tell others of the Master Carpenter who can still mend broken hearts. If you are a teacher, you will teach your students about the One who brought the truth which sets persons free. If you are a banker, you will tell your customers about spiritual reserves which they may draw on eternally if they invest their lives in Christ.

If you walk with Jesus you will find yourself saying, like the apostles, "We cannot stop speaking what we have seen and heard" (v. 20).

4. A New Picture of God (4:23-30)

After being released, the apostles gathered with the rest of the Christians to thank God for His deliverance. Their prayers reflected a new picture of God which came to them as they walked with Jesus.

Jesus gave the most beautiful picture of God that humanity has ever seen. In His incarnation, He revealed the nearness of God. In His teachings, He revealed the wisdom of God. In His relationship with people, He revealed the patience of God. On the cross, He revealed the love of God. In His resurrection, He revealed the power of God. In His second coming, He will reveal the ultimate victory of God.

The world might tempt you to think God doesn't care. Satan will tempt you to believe God is not important. Skeptics will tempt you to believe God doesn't exist. But when you walk with Jesus, you will know that God is present, that God is love, that God is power, and that God cares about you.

5. A New Power (4:31)

When the apostles prayed, the place where they were assembled was shaken with the power of God (v. 31). These pages that tell the story of the first church literally ripple with the power of God. Barriers were broken down. Illnesses were healed. Buildings were shaken. Cities were evangelized. Lives were changed. Eventually the very Roman Empire itself was brought to its knees before the resurrected Christ.

The power which made all of that possible was Jesus. The source of that power was God. The agent of that power was the Holy Spirit. The result of that power was changed lives, changed nations, and a changed world. The method by which that power was experienced was prayer. What a prayer meeting for us to emulate.

The apostles prayed *in the right context* (4:23). This was not ivory-tower praying, isolated from the realities of life. This prayer to God was rooted in service for God.

The apostles prayed *in the right spirit* (4:24). This was not self-centered prayer, focusing only on individual petitions. This was a symphony of prayer from people united in mind and spirit, "with one accord."

The apostles prayed *on the right basis* (4:25-26). This was not prayer based on personal whims. This prayer was solidly based on the Word of God. The quotation is from Psalm 2.

The apostles prayed *for the right reason* (4:27-30). This was not a vindictive prayer which requested the change in their circumstances or the destruction of their enemies. This was a prayer for power to make the most of those circumstances and to convince those enemies. These apostles did not ask for protection. They asked for power. They did not pray for easier circumstances. They prayed for stronger character to meet those circumstances.

The apostles prayed *with the right results* (4:31). Walking with Jesus will provide the power to evangelize the masses, energize the churches, vitalize Christianity, and revolutionize our society.

Living in Jesus (4:32-37)

What a spiritual mountaintop for the apostles as they celebrated their victorious encounter with the Jewish leaders. The words of the prayer of thanksgiving (4:24-30) indicate the loftiness of their thoughts. Yet, notice the ease with which they moved from the ethereal level to the practical, from the mountaintop of devotion to the valley of dedication. Devotion to God did not isolate them from the reality of problems around them. Rather, devotion to God motivated them to meet those problems in practical concern.

Nowhere do we see a more beautiful example of this attitude than in the man introduced to us in verse 36. His name was Joseph. We know him by the nickname he earned. He was called *bar nabas*—son of consolation. He was known as "Mr. Encouragement." This was not a nickname capriciously coined but one that grew out of his life. In every picture of him in the Book of Acts, Barnabas was "the encourager."

In Acts 4:36-37, Barnabas was confronted by some specific needs in the church. People were going hungry. They had no money to supply their own needs. Barnabas sold a piece of land and gave the money to the church to be used to meet those needs. This was a practical, tangible way of lending a helping hand.

In Acts 9, we see Barnabas again. Saul of Tarsus had met Christ on the Damascus road and had been converted. Saul insisted he was a Christian, but everyone in the church was suspicious of him, fearing he had feigned his faith to infiltrate the church to persecute Christians further. Everyone was suspicious of Saul except Barnabas, the encourager. Barnabas talked with Saul. Then he talked with the leaders of the church and persuaded them to accept him as a brother in Christ (v. 27).

In Acts 11, we see Barnabas again. The gospel was preached in Antioch, and many Gentiles were saved. The Jewish Christians in Jerusalem were uncertain that Gentiles could be saved without becoming Jews. They wanted to investigate what was happening in Antioch. Who was sent to investigate? Barnabas, the encourager, was sent. When he came to Antioch the Bible says, "He rejoiced and began to encourage them with resolute heart to remain true to the Lord" (v. 23).

In Acts 15, we see Barnabas encouraging another young Christian. Paul and Barnabas took John Mark with them on the first missionary journey. Along the way, Mark quit and returned home (Acts 13:13). When Paul and Barnabas made plans for a second trip, Barnabas wanted to give Mark a second chance, but Paul refused. So convinced was Barnabas that Mark was still useful to God that he and Paul separated. Paul found another partner, and Barnabas took John Mark. Once again we see Barnabas as the encourager.

Barnabas demonstrated the attitude of these first Christians as they lived in Jesus. The early church was known for the way it helped hold people together. Unfortunately, too often today the church is known for the way we pick people apart. Ours is a critical age. We are quick to see people's faults, slow to recognize their strengths. We are quick to criticize, hesitant to congratulate. The work of the church in such a world is to carry out the ministry of encouragement.

4 | The Real Thing

Acts 5:1-42

In the mining town of Holden, West Virginia, an accident trapped thirty-six miners underground. As the rescue teams emerged, soot covering their faces, the anxious relatives sought word about their family members. When the rescuers had no word, the local minister said to the people, "Let's pray." The people joined hands and began singing "What a Friend We Have in Jesus." Then the preacher prayed. A reporter from one of the national news networks wanted the scene on the evening news.

However, the cold weather had caused the camera to malfunction. So the reporter approached the minister and said, "Preacher, could you please go back through your prayer? We have over two hundred television stations across the country who will send out a picture of your prayer to millions of listeners."

The mountain preacher responded, "Son, I just couldn't do that. I've already prayed, and any other praying at this time would be put on. No sir, I just can't do that." That country preacher was so genuine in his faith he would not make a show of his religion or sell his soul to a national news agency. He was the real thing![1]

The early church was just like our churches today, a mixture of the real thing and counterfeit Christians. Both counterfeits and genuine articles are seen in this fifth chapter of the Book of Acts.

The Imposters (5:1-10)

What is the most irritating epithet someone could hurl our way? Probably we would most abhor the accusation of being a hypocrite.

More than anything else we want to be known as genuine and sincere. False claims by advertisers, false promises by politicians, and false fronts by people are all around. Ours is a day in which we desire to tell it like it is. We don't want to be called hypocrites.

Most have a deep respect for genuineness and an even deeper fear of hypocrisy. That is why, of all the villains of the Bible, none except Judas so repulses us as do these two hypocrites of the early church: Ananias and Sapphira. *Ananias* means "God is gracious," and *Sapphira* means "beautiful." Neither lived up to their names, because Ananias tested the graciousness of God, and Sapphira displayed the lack of beauty in her life.

Their story has to be understood against the backdrop of Barnabas. He saw a need, and he felt a conviction. So he followed through on that conviction and met that need. The result was a rich respect and an abundant acclaim for Barnabas. Ananias and Sapphira desired that same acclaim, but they were not motivated by the same conviction. Barnabas was motivated by the desire to meet a need. Ananias and Sapphira were motivated by the desire to receive praise. That was the difference.

Ananias and Sapphira developed a plan. They would sell some of their land, keep a part of the money for themselves, and then bring the rest to the church as an offering, claiming that it was the full purchase price for the land. As the plot unfolded, Ananias brought the money to the church. Through the Holy Spirit, Peter discovered what Ananias had done, and he confronted Ananias with it. Ananias fell dead at Peter's feet. When Sapphira came in, she too claimed that the money was the full price for the land. Peter confronted her with the awfulness of what she had done and told her what had happened to her husband, and she too fell dead.

What was the sin of Ananias and Sapphira? They claimed to be something they were not. They were hypocrites. The Greek word *hypocrite* means an actor. The role of an actor is such that from the moment one dons a mask and begins a performance, one's whole conduct on state is in keeping with an assigned role. A hypocrite is one who plays a part. This acting is reflected in two directions.

1. Convictions Not Followed

A hypocrite claims religious convictions he or she does not follow. Someone wrote of such hypocrites, "I met the strangest man the other day. He said he believes in the Bible, but he never reads it. He said he thought well of the church of which he is a member, but he never attends. He said a man should be honest with God in money matters, but he never tithes. He said the younger generation needs the Lord, but he isn't leading them in that direction. He said the church needs dedicated Christian members, but he isn't one. He said the church should do more in ministering to people, but he doesn't help. He is critical of the way the church is "run," but he never participates. He says prayer will change things, but he never prays. He was a strange man indeed."

That is a precise picture of a hypocrite, one who like Ananias and Sapphira claims conviction that one does not follow.

2. Commitments Not Felt

A hypocrite is also one who claims commitments one does not feel. Even more tragic than those who claim something but do not follow it are those who follow something but do not really feel it. Their religion is a sham. Their religious motions are void of any deep foundation within their lives. They worship, but their hearts are not in it. They punctuate their pronouncements with "praise the Lords," but there is a ring of insincerity about them.

This was the problem with Ananias and Sapphira. They claimed to have an unselfish devotion to God, they claimed to be completely sold out to Him, but in reality they still sat on the throne of their own lives. Instead of being concerned about their standing before God, they were really concerned about their status in the church. So to enhance that status, they claimed to make commitments which they did not feel.

To claim convictions but fail to follow through or claim commitments but fail to feel them is the essence of hypocrisy.

When Jesus asked, "Why do you call Me, 'Lord, Lord,' and do not do what I say?" (Luke 6:46), He was addressing those hypocrites of His age and every age who seem more religious than they are. The word we need to give to them was beautifully expressed by an old country lady who said, "Be what you is. Because if you be what you ain't, then you ain't what you be."

The Impression (5:11-16)

As the story of Ananias and Sapphira spread, a deep impression was registered both on the Christians "great fear came upon the whole church," (v. 11) and on those outside the church "upon all who heard of these things," (v. 11). Luke described the result in the life of the church.

1. Power (5:12a)

Luke said, "At the hands of the apostles many signs and wonders were taking place among the people" (v. 12). "Signs and wonders" was a stock phrase for Luke. Six other times in the Book of Acts we see these two words *signs* and *wonders* used in conjunction (2:19; 2:22; 2:43; 4:30; 7:36; and 14:3). Great things were happening in the first-century church, events so out of the ordinary that they could not be explained apart from the hand of God. These Christians felt God's power working among them. That same power which energized the New Testament church is also available to us. And it is a miracle-working power.

A pastor told a children's story one morning at the worship service. He had a sack full of acorns that he had picked up at his house. With the children gathered around him, the pastor peeked into the sack and said, "I have a miracle in this sack. How many of you children would like to hold a miracle in your hands?" All the hands shot up, of course, so he gave to each one of them an acorn. Then he told this story. God had put an oak tree in each of those acorns. Once planted in the ground, along with the warmth of the sun and the nourishment of rain, a great oak tree could grow up to produce millions of other acorns—all out of that one acorn. God has put a miracle in us. If we allow it, the miracle can grow, nurtured by the warmth of the love of others.

Later, as the people were leaving church, a mother and her son stopped before the preacher. The mother said, "Go ahead and tell the preacher."

With the greatest seriousness, the boy responded, "Preacher, I lost my miracle."[2]

Many Christians and many churches today have lost their miracles because they have quit believing in miracles. If we will allow the power of God to work in our churches and in our lives, we will experience, as the first-century church did, many signs and wonders in our midst.

2. Unity (5:12b)

The release of God's power resulted in a great sense of unity. Luke explained, "And they were all with one accord in Solomon's portico" (v. 12). Luke was not talking about uniformity where every Christian has to fit the same mold, and everybody talks, walks, and acts exactly the same. Luke was talking about unity, a unity of purpose, a unity of spirit, and a unity of direction.

A hunter was preparing his dogs for a fox hunt. They were jumping at each other and nipping at each other's heels. They were fighting among themselves. But when the hunter set the fox loose, the dogs stopped fighting and set out in unity to catch the fox. That's what happens in a church when God's power is released. The squabbling and nitpicking will stop because we will no longer be concerned about what we want. We will be concerned about what God wants.

3. Influence (5:13-16)

When God's power was released and Christians moved forward with a unity of purpose, they had a strong, positive influence on those around them. Luke's summary statement seems confusing. When Luke said, "But none of the rest dared to associate with them" (v. 13), he was referring to those who, like Ananias and Sapphira, were trying to fake the faith. The people in general, however, had a deep respect for the Christians. Luke told us that the mere shadow of

Peter falling across them had a positive effect on their lives (v. 15).

Luke was saying that genuine, enthusiastic faith is contagious. A Christian who is for real will convince others that God is for real. A church which is on fire will set the community on fire. Genuine faith is contagious.

The Imprisonment (5:17-33)

Because of the tremendous influence the church was exerting on the people, the religious leaders became alarmed. The high priest and the Sadducees "were filled with jealousy" (v. 17). Why would the Sadducees be alarmed? One problem was the Christian message, a message which focused on the resurrection of Jesus Christ (Acts 4:33). The Sadducees did not believe in the resurrection and were thus threatened by the message of the apostles. Perhaps more serious was the provocation of the people caused by the apostles. Maintaining the status quo was essential to the political power wielded by the Sadducees. Any threat of rebellion had to be squelched. Therefore, the apostles were arrested and put in jail (5:18).

1. The Deliverance (5:19-26)

The apostles were not even settled down in the jail when an angel of the Lord appeared. The angel released them from the cell and ordered them to again declare the gospel. The next morning the Sanhedrin met to decide what to do with these followers of Jesus. When they sent for the apostles, the officer reported that the apostles were gone. Perplexity turned to anguish when another messenger came with the report that they were back in the temple preaching. The officers of the court picked up the apostles again and brought them before the Sanhedrin.

2. The Declaration (5:27-32)

Standing before the Sanhedrin, Peter declared the same message. We see the allusion to the Old Testament background in the phrase: "The God of our fathers" (v. 30). We see the brief analysis of Jesus' life in the phrase: "whom you had put to death by hanging Him on a cross" (v. 30). We see the affirmation of who Jesus is in the phrase: "He is the one whom God exalted to His right hand as a Prince and a Savior" (v. 31). Peter then promised forgiveness and the Holy Spirit to those who believed (v. 32).

The Sanhedrin reacted with animosity and hostility. Their plan was to put the apostles to death. Again, God intervened by raising up a strange ally, a man by the name of Gamaliel.

The Intervention (5:34-40)

Gamaliel was likely the grandson of the famous rabbi Hillel who along with Shammai headed the two great schools of Pharisaic thought. Gamaliel stood in the liberal tradition of his grandfather for his liberality was reflected in his gracious attitude toward others. So great was the influence of Gamaliel that one Jewish tradition declared, "Since Rabban Gamaliel died there has been no more reverence for the Law; and purity and abstinence died out at the same time."[3] Yet, for all his graciousness of spirit and all his beauty of character, what has made Gamaliel's fame endure across the centuries is the speech he made in defense of the first Christians.

The Sanhedrin was ready to put the Christians to death (v. 33). At that point, Gamaliel intervened. Gamaliel reminded the Sanhedrin of two revolutionaries who stirred up a rebellion but whose uprisings were quickly snuffed out (vv. 35-37). The heart of Gamaliel's defense is found in verses 38-39. He suggested caution, for as he put it, this might be the hand of God at work. Gamaliel appealed for three things.

1. Time

We all know time is the great healer. Cut yourself seriously, and the pain is intense. But as the days go by, time has a healing effect, and soon there is nothing left but a scar to remind you of your pain.

Time is also a great revealer. Things are not always what they seem to be. Immediate evaluations are not always accurate. It is often necessary for enough time to pass to enable us to get a broader perspective before we can evaluate an experience accurately.

Gamaliel warned the Sanhedrin not to criticize or to condemn the Christian movement until they had given it time to show itself for what it really is.

2. Truth

As is so often the case with us, the members of the Sanhedrin lost sight of the real issue. The members of the Sanhedrin were concerned about *their feelings.* When they were "cut to the quick" (5:33), they began to make plans to kill the apostles. Their feelings condemned the apostles. Gamaliel reminded them that their feelings were not the issue.

The members of the Sanhedrin were also concerned about *their positions.* They were the religious teachers. Yet, here were untrained men without proper credentials who were usurping their positions. They could sense their power slipping away. No longer were they in charge. No longer were they calling the shots. They were in danger, so they wanted to put the Christians away. Gamaliel reminded them that their positions were not the issue.

In addition, the members of the Sanhedrin were concerned about *their understanding.* Their neat little doctrinal package was being shattered. These Christians were rocking the boat, so the Sanhedrin wanted to destroy them. Gamaliel reminded them that their understanding was not the issue.

What then was the issue? Gamaliel said the issue was the truth. That must always be the issue for us as Christians. That must always be our heartfelt desire: not that our feelings be projected, not that our position be maintained, not that our understanding be confirmed, but that we might discover the truth.

3. Tolerance

We often use a different standard of judgment for others than we do for ourselves. We often put the best light on what we do and the worse light on others. When others take a long time to do something, they are slow. But when we take a long time to do something, we're thorough. When others don't do something, they are too lazy. When we don't do it, we're too busy. When others go ahead and do something without being told, they're overstepping their bounds. But when we go ahead and do something without being told, that's initiative. When others state their side of the question strongly, they're bullheaded. But when we state our side of a question strongly, we're standing up for our own rights. When others overlook a few rules of etiquette, they're rude. But when we skip a few rules of etiquette, we're free spirits. When others do something that pleases the boss, they're polishing brass. But when we do something that pleases the boss, that's cooperation. When others get ahead, they sure had the lucky breaks. But when we manage to get ahead, our hard work was the key. This tendency to be tolerant toward ourselves and intolerant toward others leads to a spirit of censoriousness that more that any other one single factor decimates the fellowship of the church and undermines its effectiveness.

In the speech that made him famous, Gamaliel urged a spirit of tolerance. This is not a spineless acceptance of everything but an attitude that is willing to evaluate others in the same light that we evaluate ourselves.

The Implications (5:41-42)

In the summary statement in the closing verses of the chapter, Luke revealed two implications of the events described in this chapter.

1. Their Mission (5:41)

In our day of convenient Christianity, cheap grace, and the comfortable pew, the attitude of these first Christians expressed in this verse is almost beyond comprehension. These Christians had been "flogged" (Acts 5:40). This probably means they were each given thirty-nine strokes on their backs. How did they respond? Luke said, "So they went on their way from the presence of the Council, rejoicing that they had been considered worthy to suffer shame for His name" (5:41). We look for the easy way out. These first Christians thanked God they could take the hard way. We ask, "How little can we give?" These first Christians thanked God they had the opportunity to give so much.

We do sacrifice at times today for the sake of vocational success, for the sake of personal achievement, for the sake of good health, and sometimes, for the sake of family. But sacrifice for the name of Christ, sacrifice in the spiritual realm, is rare. However, at the heart of the Christian faith is a Man hanging on a cross. And that Man called His followers not to a life of comfort but to a life of sacrifice.

We see the *motivation for sacrifice.* The motivation for the sacrificial life is the Man named Jesus, who died on the cross, was raised from the dead in the power of God, and now has been exalted to the right hand of the Father as the Lord of all life. Because He says to come and follow Him, because He says to take up our crosses, and because He calls us to sacrifice, we obey.

A. W. Tozer once said, "It is not what a man does that determines if it is sacred or secular—it is why he does it."[4] The Christian is willing to sacrifice because of love for Jesus. We see in this verse the *meaning of sacrifice. Sacrifice* means that it costs to be a Christian.

When he preached in one of the Iron Curtain countries, Lewis Drummond told of a young woman who came forward for counseling, but she did not seem serious about the decision. Dr. Drummond and the local pastor dismissed her and moved to other counselees. When they had finished, the young woman was still there. They counseled with her again, and she received Christ. After the prayer of commitment, she asked what happens if a Christian sins. The native pastor talked with her and discovered she was in a certain situation where if she told the truth about a particular happening, she would have to make a real sacrifice. If she could lie, she would be safe. The question she was asking was this: Can a person be a Christian and play it safe? Dr. Drummond explained that a Christian is one who follows Christ regardless of the sacrifice demanded. For a few moments the young woman did not speak. Finally, with tears in her eyes, she said to the pastor, "I'll do the will of God no matter what it costs."[5]

2. Their Message (5:42)

In a day when many messages are sent out across our land, we need to hear again the message of the first Christians: "Every day, in the temple and from house to house, they kept right on teaching and preaching Jesus as the Christ" (5:42).

In a little town in Sweden, an unusual crucifix hangs on the pillar opposite the pulpit. The crucifix was a special gift to the church from King Charles XII. He visited the church in 1716. The visit was unexpected and created quite a stir. When the pastor saw the king walking up the path to the church, he threw aside his prepared sermon and instead gave a tribute to the king and his family. A few months later the church received from the king a crucifix with these instructions: "This is to hang on the pillar opposite the pulpit so that whoever stands there will be reminded of his proper subject."[6] The power of yesterday's church and the hope of today's church is that we keep teaching and preaching Jesus Christ.

The first Christians preached Jesus as the *Lamb* (John 1:29; 1 Pet. 1:19; and Rev. 5:12). What did this mean? The Lamb was the perfect sacrifice that was laid upon the altar of the cross to cover the sins of the world.

The first Christians preached Jesus as the *Life* (John 5:24; John 6:33; and John 10:10). What did this mean? In Jesus, we have a purpose to live for, a power to live by, and a person to live with. Jesus not only saves us from our sins. He saves us for a new life.

The first Christians preached Jesus as the *Lord* (2 Cor. 4:5; Rom. 1:4; and Acts 2:36). What did this mean? The Lord of a house was in charge of the house. The Lord of a nation was in charge of the nation. To call Jesus Lord means He is in charge of our lives. He calls the shots. He gives the directions. He makes the decisions. Because He is Lord, we are His servants. Because He is Lord, we obey Him.

The message of the church must always be the good news about Jesus Christ. He, and He alone, is our proper subject.

5 | Organizing for Effectiveness

Acts 6:1-7

At no other time in Christian history has the church of Jesus Christ been characterized by the phenomenal growth, the marvelous miracles, the pulsating power, the undaunted boldness, and the unlimited favor which it experienced in these first weeks and months of its existence. Yet, right in the middle of the stupendous success story, we learn of a dissension that endangered the entire mission of the church. As we read the sixth chapter of the Book of Acts we make a surprising discovery. The church of the first century was not perfect. Instead, it was very much like our churches are today, made up of less-than-perfect people who knew the reality of practical problems, petty attitudes, and perplexing issues.

There are no perfect churches because churches are made up of people, and there are no perfect people. To call a new preacher will not make a church perfect. To elect new deacons will not make a church perfect. To construct a new building will not make a church perfect. To change locations will not make a church perfect. To adopt new programs will not make a church perfect. There are no perfect churches. This fact which I have discovered experientially and which I believe intellectually is affirmed biblically in the sixth chapter of the Book of Acts. This less-than-perfect New Testament church, nevertheless, was experiencing tremendous growth. As the church grew, these first Christians faced the challenge of organizing for effectiveness.

The Problem (6:1)

Evidently, a considerable time lapsed between chapter 5 and chapter 6. During this time, the church had grown rapidly. Instead of adding new members to the church (Acts 2:41,47), Luke said the number of disciples was multiplying (v. 1). It was a time of rapid growth in the church. Two different kinds of people were joining the church.

Among those joining the church were "Hellenistic Jews." These were Jews who spoke Greek as their basic language and who had been influenced by Greek culture. These were probably Jews of the Dispersion who had lived in parts of the world where the Greek influence was dominant and who now, either temporarily or permanently, were dwelling in Jerusalem.

Also among those joining the church were "native Hebrews." These were people who spoke Aramaic as their basic language and who were influenced by a different culture than the Hellenists. They grew up in Palestine and were Hebrews in every way.

The problem which erupted in the church revolved around these two groups. In the distribution of the food which had been given to the church, the Hellenists felt they were being mistreated. So here in the most exciting moment in the history of the church, when God's power was being felt, and when the church was multiplying in size, a dissension arose among the people. Let me try to translate the problem in terms of today's church.

1. Quantity Versus Quality

The quantity of additions to the church was affecting the quality of the fellowship. The success of the church was actually the source of the problem in the church. Some in the church were saying, "We're getting so big we're losing sight of the individual."

That conflict has reappeared in history many times. Whenever a church grows, new members are added, and new leadership is enlisted. Some will complain, "We don't need to reach more people. We just need to take care of the ones we have. We're big enough." Quantity versus quality!

2. My Group Versus Your Group

The Western Text of the New Testament adds an interesting clause to the end of verse 1. It says that the Hellenists complained about being overlooked in the distribution of food "because it was being administered by Hebrews." The problem arose because one group did not like the way the other group was doing things.

Lyle Schaller suggested this is still very much a problem today. He said that in every organization any unsolicited idea that comes in from the outside tends to be rejected. He quoted one man as saying, "In the research lab where I work we called that NIH—not invented here."[1] My group verses your group!

3. Evangelism Versus Edification

What is the purpose of the church? Some say, "It is evangelism. Our sole responsibility is to win people to Christ."

"No," say others, "there is more to our purpose than that. We are not simply to win converts. We are to make disciples. Edification, or building up the believers, that is our major task." Over the centuries Christians have continued to debate the relative merits of evangelism and edification oblivious to the fact that these are not two independent entities but two aspects of the same task, two sides of the same coin. Our evangelism and edification must go hand in hand. This was the question which rocked the early church: evangelism versus edification.

When I read Acts 6, I was encouraged to discover that even in the first-century church, made up of men and women who had sat at Jesus' feet, there were some problems. In the problem described in Acts 6 we see the foreshadowing of some of the most perplexing problems which have confronted the church in every age: the problem of quantity versus quality, the problem of my group versus your group, and the problem of evangelism versus edification.

The Procedure (6:2-4)

What procedure did the apostles use to deal with the problem? Note what they did not do.

1. Ignore the Problem

They did not ignore the problem, thinking that somehow it would just go away. Of course, some problems which are not real problems will simply go away if we give them enough time. However, when a problem reaches the proportion that this one did in the early church, it will not solve itself. We must deal with it.

A group of college boys wanted to keep the football team mascot— a goat. They made intricate plans to smuggle the animal into their dormitory room. Someone asked, "But what about the smell?"

The others replied, "The goat will just have to get used to it!" The apostles did not just get used to the problem.

2. Resent the Problem

Neither did the apostles resent the problem. They could have taken the criticism personally and reacted with resentment. "After all," they could have said, "who are you to tell us how to serve bread? We are experts at it. Have you forgotten that we were with Jesus when He fed the 5,000? Do you not remember that we were with Jesus when He broke bread at the last Passover feast? We know all about serving bread." They did not deal with the problem in that way.

Whistler's name is famous today as a great artist. However, he had his critics in his day. Whistler was unhappy when others criticized his work. He even sued one critic who accused him of "flinging a pot of paint in the public's face." After seeing the finished portrait done by Whistler, his subject protested, "You can't call that a great work of art." Whistler responded, "Perhaps not, but then you can't call yourself a great work of nature!"[2] The apostles did not react to the problem like that.

3. Overreact to the Problem

Notice also they did not overreact to the problem. Sometimes we overreact to criticism by yielding to it before testing its validity and thus compound our problems. The apostles did not do this. They did not quit seeking quantity just because there was some question about the quality of the fellowship. They were concerned with both. They did not ignore the Hebrews now just to keep the Hellenists from complaining. They were concerned with both. They did not give up evangelism in favor of edification. They were concerned with both. They did not try to solve one problem by introducing others. We never solve a wrong with another wrong. Instead, we must replace the wrong with a right.

A farmer was plowing his corn one hot day when he heard a scratching sound. He saw a mouse gnawing away at a stalk of corn. He thought of the long hours spent clearing the field, planting it, and cultivating it, and now this mouse was trying to destroy it. In his anger, the farmer picked up a stick and went after the mouse. He beat, slashed, chased, and sweated until finally he dealt the mouse a lethal blow. He felt a deep sense of satisfaction until he looked around and realized he had destroyed nearly half an acre of corn to kill one little mouse. The apostles did not respond to their problem like that.

4. Face the Problem

What then did the apostles do? With what procedure did they handle the problem? They decided what the problem was, and then they determined a course of action to take care of it. Simply put, they divided the responsibilities and enlisted sufficient personnel to carry out those responsibilities. They selected seven men to serve the tables and care for the widows, seven men who were especially equipped to carry out this ministry in a loving and skillful way, and then the apostles dedicated themselves to what they could do best: praying and preaching the Word.

With this procedure, the apostles highlighted a key New Testament concept—the idea of spiritual gifts in the body of Christ. The church is like a body made up of different parts empowered to carry out different functions. The church is most healthy and productive when each part of the body is carrying out its proper function. The work of the New Testament church is not a one-man show. God's work will not be accomplished by a handful of the elite. This church continued to advance when those who were gifted to preach continued to preach and when those who were gifted to wait on tables waited on tables. As each used his gift, the body of Christ moved forward.

The People (6:3-5)

To solve the problem, the apostles led the church to select seven men. This was the initial step in organizing the church for effectiveness.

1. The Qualification

They were to be men of *integrity*. Luke called them "men of good reputation" (v. 3) Henry Clay, a perennial candidate for president of the United States, took an unpopular stand on an issue of great importance to him. His advisors told him, "Henry, if you take this position, you will never be President of the United States." Clay responded, "I'd rather be right than be President."[3] That's integrity, the willingness to stand up for what is right instead of what is convenient or popular.

They were to be men of *infilling*. The men selected for this special assignment in the church were to be "full of the Spirit" (v. 3). Some say that a leader "really has charisma." On other occasions, we may speak of someone as being charismatic. The key to effective leadership in the church is not that we be charismatic but that we be pneumatic—filled with the Spirit.

They were to be men of *intelligence*. Luke said they were also to be full "of wisdom" (v. 3). One of the great biblical preachers in Christian history was G. Campbell Morgan of England. His impact on the people of Leicester was registered in the local paper. The reporter said about Morgan,

> Leicester has been experiencing grand times sitting at the feet of the greatest living exponent of the Scriptures, the Rev. Dr. Campbell Morgan. . . . One does not have to listen to Dr. Morgan long without realizing wherein lies his attractive power. One does not know whether to describe it as his spiritual intellectuality or his intellectual spirituality, but the attractiveness is certainly compounded out of a great brain and a great soul.[4]

That description fits these men selected by the first church for special assignment. They combined "a great brain and a great soul." They were "full of the Spirit and of wisdom."

2. The Designation

We refer to these as the first deacons, but were they? The noun *diakonia* later used to designate deacons is used in verse 1. However, it does not refer to a person but to a function—the administration of the food. The verb *diakonein* also appears in verse 2 and is translated "serve." Tradition and the emphasis on service in this passage allows us to speak of these as the first deacons of the church.

The word used to designate a deacon clearly explains the work of the deacon. Deacons are set aside to be servants. A minister once visited Mother Teresa, the woman who ministers to the dying on the streets of Calcutta. He was amazed at the evident joy in Mother Teresa's life. He asked her, "How do you do this awful work?"

She responded, "Awful work? What do you mean? I'm immensely privileged. I'm serving my Lord—tangibly."[5]

That was the work of these first deacons: to serve the Lord tangibly. They were to wait on tables and administer the distribution of the food.

The Product (6:7)

Notice the positive results which followed the action of the apostles.

1. The Problem Solved

No other mention is ever made of this particular problem in the New Testament. They faced the problem and dealt with it. The needs of the congregation were met, and the problem was solved. Luke said, "The statement found approval with the whole congregation" (v. 5).

2. The Gifts Activated

These seven men were not ministers. They were not preachers. They were laymen. Yet, they had been given gifts of ministry by the Holy Spirit. The Bible makes this clear in 1 Corinthians 12:4-11. When these gifts of the Spirit were activated and utilized, the problem was solved.

To every one of us God has given a special gift to be used in carrying out the ministry of the church. When we activate those gifts and utilize them in the life of the church, every problem will simply be a stepping-stone to further achievement.

3. The Apostles Liberated

The apostles were now able to give their full attention to the priorities God had set before them—praying and preaching. Often, in today's church, the pastors get so bogged down in problem-solving that they are diverted from the priorities of their ministry, one of which is to preach the Word. On the other hand, when the lay people who have the gifts, wisdom, and resources to deal with the daily problems that emerge in the life of the church and when the pastor is thus freed to give his full attention to preparing himself spiritually and preaching the Word of God with power, then watch out! Exciting things are going to happen.

4. The Church Unified

Since everyone was busy at the Lord's work—the laity doing what the laity were gifted to do, and the apostles doing what they were gifted to do—everyone was busy doing the Lord's work, and they had no time for argument and bickering. Consequently, the divisiveness was replaced by unity.

Since the problem was solved, the gifts of the laity were activated, the apostles were liberated to do their work, and the church was unified, the result was growth. Luke said, "The word of God kept on spreading, the number of the disciples continued to increase greatly in Jerusalem, and a great many of the priests were becoming obedient to the faith" (v. 7).

The Principles

Two principles for effective Christian work are demonstrated in this experience.

1. Organization

In writing to the Corinthians, Paul gave this command: "But let all things be done properly and in an orderly manner" (1 Cor. 14:40). Paul was applying a basic truth to the work of the church; organization is a key to effectiveness.

In September 1989, there was a Billy Graham Crusade in Little Rock, Arkansas. For eight nights the Billy Graham team led crusade services at War Memorial Stadium. During those eight days, 282,800 attended the crusade, and 6,677 decisions were registered. How did it happen? The key was the organization by the Billy Graham team. One year before the crusade, Billy Graham sent his staff to Little Rock to begin the organizational process. Twenty-five members served on an executive committee that met every month for a year. Thousands of Christians in the city were involved in training to be counselors and ushers. An organized enrollment plan brought four thousand people to sing in the choir. The organization of God's people provided the framework for the effectiveness of the week.

2. Cooperation

The writer of Ecclesiastes declared, "Two are better than one because they have a good return for their labor. For if either of them falls, the one will lift up his companion. But woe to the one who falls when there is not another to lift him up" (4:9-10). This truth applies to the work of God in the church as well as it does to any other group.

Organization only provides the opportunity for effectiveness. Effectiveness is realized through cooperation.

In the early church, deacons cooperated with apostles, men cooperated with women, and Jews eventually cooperated with Gentiles. Each was important, and all were necessary. The result was growth in effectiveness, influence, and numbers.

A retired pastor was asked by a young man to describe what it's like to be a pastor. The old saint replied, "I went through three stages in my understanding. During my early days, I pictured the congregation in the water, going down for the third time. I was standing on the shore, telling them how they could get from where they were to where I was. Then, after a few years, I developed a different picture. The people were still in the water, still going under for the third time. However, I pictured me as standing on the edge of the water with one foot on dry land and one foot in the water, reaching out to help them get in from where they were to where I was. Finally, after years in the ministry, I came to a true understanding of what it is like. Now I understand that I am in the water. And the people are holding me up. And underneath us all are the everlasting arms of God."[6]

That's the picture of the first church presented in Acts 6. The apostles were held up by the deacons, the deacons by the people, and underneath them all were the everlasting arms of God. Organization provided the opportunity for effectiveness. Cooperation made it happen.

6 Deacons at Work

Acts 6:8—8:40

The teenager came out of the witness training class with a real burden to share the gospel with everyone he saw. He approached a man after church and said, "I want to know, sir, if you are saved."

The man replied, "I'll have you know I'm a deacon."

The boy replied, "That's all right. My teacher told me God could forgive anything!"

Some deacons in the church do not "deac." They have stood in the way of the work of God rather than furthering God's work. For example, the preacher called for a vote on an issue which gained the approval of the majority. He said to the congregation, "Let's take the vote again and make it unanimous."

One old deacon stood up and said, "Preacher, as long as I'm in this church there ain't going to be anything unanimous."

On the other hand, dedicated deacons over the centuries have been vital contributors to the expansion of God's kingdom. Stephen and Philip would fit in that category. They show us what happens when deacons go to work.

Stephen (6:8—7:60)

Billy Graham was in India several years ago for a crusade. While he was there he witnessed to a man about Christ and then asked him if he would become a Christian. The man gave this response: "I like what you have said. If I ever see a real Christian I will become one."

Billy Graham said, "The most tragic aspect about the man's response was that he was looking at me when he said it."

Many people in our world today say the same thing. If they could ever see a real Christian, they would become one. Of all the descriptions that could be given of Stephen—the first deacon, an eloquent preacher of the gospel, an effective witness, and the first Christian martyr—perhaps none is as accurate as to say Stephen was a real Christian. Notice the characteristics of his life revealed in this biographical sketch in Acts 6—7.

1. His Character (6:5)

The apostles told the congregation to select seven men "of good reputation, full of the Spirit and of wisdom" who could deal with the problem that had arisen in the church (v. 3). The problem was so serious it could have irrevocably divided the church. The future of the gospel was at stake. Therefore, key men had to be called out to take care of the problem; men whose reputations were beyond question and whose common sense would ensure the proper disposition of the problem. Stephen was one of those chosen. He is described as a man "full of faith and of the Holy Spirit" (v. 5).

Stephen was *full of faith*. *Full of faith* means Stephen held nothing back from God. His life was completely yielded to the will of God as revealed in Jesus Christ. How different from the rich young ruler described in Luke 18 whom Jesus met one day. He, too, was a fine young man with tremendous capabilities, but there was something he would not yield to Christ, a part of his life he would not release. The heartbreaking testimony of Jesus as this rich young ruler walked away was, "One thing you still lack" (Luke 18:22).

That is the testimony of many Christians today: One sin retained, and all the rest of our lives dimmed in consequence. One corner of our lives barricaded against Christ, and all the rest reduced in its effectiveness. One moral compromise accepted, and the full blessing of God never known. In contrast, Stephen was a man who was willing to yield all of his life to God. He was a man "full of faith."

Stephen was also *full of the Spirit*. To be "full of the Spirit" means to live under the Spirit's control and be empowered with a divine dynamic that enables us to experience God's best for our lives. The

Bible says Stephen was "full . . . of the Holy Spirit."

The Holy Spirit is the key to the Christian life. The Holy Spirit will guide us into all truth (John 16:13). The Holy Spirit will comfort us in times of need (John 14:16). The Holy Spirit will tell us what to say (Rom. 8:26). The Holy Spirit will give us power (Acts 1:8). The Holy Spirit will produce in our lives that great list of benefits mentioned in Galatians 5:22: love, joy, peace, patience, kindness, goodness, faithfulness, gentleness, and self-control. A Christian cannot live without the Holy Spirit.

Stephen was a man whose character was developed because he was full of faith (willing to empty himself for Christ's sake) and full of the Holy Spirit (willing to be controlled by the power and purpose of God).

2. His Compulsion (6:8)

"Stephen, full of grace and power, was performing great wonders and signs among the people" (v. 8). What was Stephen set aside to do? To wait on tables. What was he doing? He was preaching and sharing the word of Christ with great power. No indication is given that he neglected his initial assignment. No further mention is made in the Jerusalem church of the problem which prompted the selection of these first deacons, so evidently they adequately took care of the problem.

The point is that Stephen was not satisfied in having just one assignment. He was not willing to simply do one job. He was compelled by his desire to serve God to take the initiative in finding new and wider areas of service. Stephen didn't have to receive a letter from the pastor to encourage him. He didn't have to have a special Sunday set aside for him to get excited. He didn't have to see the crowd going with him to move forward. He didn't have to be patted on the back to keep going. He took the initiative himself. He was compelled by his character to expand his service for Jesus Christ. Not external coercion but internal compulsion was the secret of Stephen's life.

When Bud Wilkinson, former football coach of the University of Oklahoma, traveled across the United States several years ago delivering lectures on physical fitness, a reporter in Dallas, Texas, interviewed him. The man asked, "Mr. Wilkinson, what would you say is the contribution of modern football to physical fitness?"

Wilkinson answered, "Absolutely nothing."

Shocked by the answer, the reporter did not know exactly what to say. Finally, he muttered, "Would you care to elaborate on that statement?"

"Certainly," Coach Wilkinson said. "I define football as 22 men on the field who desperately need rest and 50,000 people in the grandstands who desperately need exercise."

What a picture of the church: A few compulsively active people running around the field while the mass of people rest comfortably in their pews. How we need more people like Stephen in today's church who will not only develop the character needed to be used by God but will also have the compulsion to get out of the grandstand and into the game.

3. His Countenance (6:15)

Luke said, "And fixing their gaze on him, all who were sitting in the Council saw his face like the face of an angel" (v. 15). Such a glow emanated from Stephen's face and an effervescent radiance exuded from his countenance that those standing around could see the very presence of God in his face.

This was not the first time this happened to an individual in the Bible. Moses' face glowed when he came down from Mount Sinai. The Bible says, "The skin of his face shone" (Ex. 34:29). Jesus' face glowed on the mount of transfiguration. The Bible says His entire appearance was transformed, and He stood before them like a dazzling white light. "He was transfigured before them; and his face shone like the sun" (Matt. 17:2).

What happened to Stephen, Moses, and Jesus? Why the shining, radiant countenance? Because they had gone up on the mountain of prayer, away from the world, alone with God, and they had caught the rays of His glory so that their character and even their faces shone with the glory they had beheld. That was what Luke said. Stephen was in communion with God. Even at this moment of tragedy, Stephen was praying, and as he prayed, he caught the presence of God so that it was reflected on his face. How we need to be like Stephen who had spent so much time in holy communion with God that people could see God when they looked at him.

Warren Wiersbe offered an interesting insight. The members of the Sanhedrin who opposed Stephen were familiar with the fact that Moses' face shone. Perhaps God was trying to tell them, "Stephen is not against Moses. His face is shining just like Moses' face because he too is My faithful servant."[1]

4. His Comprehension (7:2-53)

Beginning in Acts 7:2, Stephen gave a summary of Old Testament history, hitting the high points, accurately tying together the work of God among His chosen people, and then relating it to the present experience of Jesus Christ. This was not a prepared sermon. This was not a message Stephen had worked on and carefully rephrased over a period of several months. This was a spontaneous, extemporaneous expression of the knowledge of God's Word which he had stored in his mind over a long period of careful study.

Stephen reviewed the contribution of Abraham (vv. 2-8), Joseph (vv. 9-17), Moses (vv. 18-44), Joshua (v. 45), and David and Solomon (vv. 46-50). Stephen then turned from review to rebuke (vv. 51-53). Stephen accused the religious leaders of repeating the folly of their ancestors. As their ancestors resisted God's prophets, they resisted God's Messiah. Stephen's message was a matchless exposition of the Scripture. Stephen was a man who knew the Word of God.

We can attend all the church services. We can serve on all the important church committees. Yet, we will never be the kind of Christian who can motivate people for the Master until we devote ourselves to the study of God's Word so that we can comprehend it, apply it to our lives, and share it with others.

5. His Courage (7:54-60)

The story reaches a climax in verse 54: "Now when they heard this, they were cut to the quick, and they began gnashing their teeth at him. But being full of the Holy Spirit, he gazed intently into heaven and saw the glory of God, and Jesus standing at the right hand of God." Up to this point the situation was calm. The people were listening to what Stephen was saying. Everything was calm. Suddenly, the scene dramatically changed. The people were ready to drag Stephen out to the streets and stone him. Still, he kept his eyes intently on Jesus. Stephen not only displayed character in times of calm, but he also displayed character in the crucible experience of his life.

To be faithful when we are in the majority, when we are on the winning side, and when our actions will bring favorable response—to be faithful when everything is going our way—that is one thing. To be faithful when people have us in their grip, when they gnash their teeth against us, and are ready to kill us, that's something else. Stephen was a man who had the courage to be consistent in his commitment, even if his commitment led to his death.

Charles G. Finney's biographer summarized his life in this sentence: "A conventional man, using conventional means is God's conventional method for bringing a fresh impulse toward heaven." How we need conventional men like Stephen who will use conventional means to let God do some unconventional things through our lives. How we need men and women who will dare to let God explode their capabilities into mighty service for Him.

Interlude (8:1-3)

In the aftermath of the Stephen episode, the church was confronted by persecution. What had happened up to this point was mild compared to the new outburst of opposition to the church. The Pharisees took the lead in this new wave of persecution. Previously, the Sadducees were most upset because of the message of the resurrection and because of the danger of a revolt breaking out. Why did the Pharisees suddenly become involved in the persecution? The key was

Stephen's message. The Pharisees were committed to the strict observance of the law. Legalism was their name, and separatism was their game. To such a group, the implications of Stephen's message were unacceptable. His emphasis on humanity as being above nation or race was too much for the Pharisees. They could not tolerate the obliteration of the distinction between Jews and Gentiles. Their entire system was based on that distinction.

A man named Saul took the lead in this new persecution. Saul "laid waste" (ASV) the church (v. 3). The word carries the connotation of a wild beast tearing his victim to shreds. This new wave of persecution was intense and destructive.

What was the result of this persecution? Ironically, the result was positive. As a result of this persecution the Christians "were all scattered throughout the regions of Judea and Samaria" (v. 1), and "those who had been scattered went about preaching the word" (v. 4). Out of persecution, the church was motivated to break through more barriers in its quest for worldwide acceptance. A great tragedy for the church became a tool by which the gospel was spread. Persecution led to expansion. Death led to new life. Fleeing Christians became willing witnesses. And this persecution which at the time seemed to herald the demise of the church was the very thing which caused its growth.

Philip (8:4-40)

One of the ones scattered was Philip, one of the first deacons of the church. When Luke said, "Philip went down to the city of Samaria, and preached Christ unto them" (v. 5, KJV), he was starting a new chapter of the history of the first-century church. Up to this point Christianity was strictly a Jewish movement. Now, Philip deliberately preached the gospel to the Samaritans.

Who were these Samaritans? When Assyria conquered the Northern Kingdom of Israel in the eighth century B.C., they deported a great part of the population from the land and replaced them with strangers from other countries. The Jews who remained in the Northern Kingdom intermarried with the strangers. The people in this resulting mixed race were called Samaritans. The deported Jews who later returned to the land refused to relate to the Samaritans. The Jews considered them half-breeds. From that day forward, a bitter breach existed between the Jews and the Samaritans. Philip challenged that traditional separation when he preached the gospel to the Samaritans. He believed they were included in the scope of Jesus' love.

1. The Message (8:4-8)

When Philip went out, he went with a message. Luke described the message: "Philip went down to the city of Samaria and began proclaiming Christ to them" (v. 5). Philip preached, "The good news about the kingdom of God and the name of Jesus Christ" (v. 12). Philip was a man with a message. That's why things were happening in Acts 8. That's why Philip was doing great miracles (v. 6). That's why there was great joy in the city (v. 8). That's why the Ethiopian eunuch went his way rejoicing (v. 39). Because Philip was proclaiming the message of Jesus Christ.

Often we talk to people about everything except the one thing they most need to hear—the power of Jesus to change their lives. Our churches will not save people, only Jesus. The personality of our leaders will not bring lost people to God, only Jesus. The programs of our churches will not lead people to eternal life, only Jesus. Jesus is the One who, if lifted up, will draw all men and women to Himself.

Like Philip, we need to hold Jesus up before the world and say, "If sin is your problem, He is forgiveness. If weakness is your problem, He is power. If lustfulness is your problem, He is purity. If fear is your problem, He is courage. If hatred is your problem, He is love. If despair is your problem, He is hope."

We do not have many messages to proclaim to the world today. We have one, and that message is about Jesus. Nothing is going to happen in our churches today unless we, like Philip, dare to go out into the world and proclaim that message.

2. The Ministry (8:9-40)

Out of Philip's ministry in Samaria, Luke isolated two incidents for closer inspection: Philip's ministry with Simon the magician and Philip's ministry with the Ethiopian eunuch.

Luke described Philip's ministry with Simon the magician (vv. 9-24). Who was Simon? Simon was a magician who was enthralled by the power of Philip. As Ananias and Sapphira tried to counterfeit the generosity of Barnabas, Simon tried to counterfeit the power of Philip. He did not want to accept Jesus. He wanted to use Jesus. We see several things about Simon.

First, we see Simon's *conception*. "Now when Simon saw that the Spirit was bestowed through the laying on of the apostles' hands, he offered them money" (v. 18). Simon saw Christianity as something he could use and the spiritual power of the apostles as something he could buy. However, spiritual power is something money cannot buy. Spiritual power comes as a result of a personal relationship with Christ.

Second, we see Simon's *condition*. Peter told Simon, "You have no part or portion in this matter, for your heart is not right before God" (v. 21). Some have questioned Luke's statement that Simon believed and was baptized (v. 13). Interpreted in the context of the passage, this faith of Simon was revealed to be a false faith. His was not a real commitment to Jesus but a false commitment to try to tap the power Jesus made available. He never really gave his heart to Jesus. Simon's faith was fake.

Third, we Simon's *concern*. Simon responded to Peter's condemnation: "Pray to the Lord for me yourselves, so that nothing of what you have said may come upon me" (v. 24). Notice Simon's concern was still centered on self. In the beginning, Simon wanted power so that he could exalt himself. Now, Simon wanted to avoid the punishment so that he could spare himself. His focus was on self.

What was the point of the Simon incident? Luke wanted to show that the power of God was superior to any other power.

Luke also described Philip's ministry with the Ethiopian eunuch

(vv. 25-40). Let's answer some questions about this experience.

Where was the Gaza road? Luke called it "a desert road" (v. 26). This phrase describes the location of the road, not its level of traffic. This was the main road south to Egypt, a road over which Barclay claimed "half the world" traveled.[2]

Who was the Ethiopian? He is called "a court official of Candace, queen of the Ethiopians, who was in charge of all her treasure" (v. 27). The Ethiopian queens were called Candace as the Egyptian rulers were called Pharaoh. This man was a high-ranking official in the Ethiopian government.

Why had this Ethiopian been in Jerusalem? Luke said he came "to worship" (v. 27). Many in that day were drawn to Judaism because of its emphasis on one God and because of its high ethical standards. Whether this man had actually converted to Judaism or was just interested in it, we do not know. He did display a strong interest in Scripture.

What happened to him on the Gaza road? The Ethiopian was converted. He became a believer in the Lord Jesus Christ. Notice the steps involved in his conversion.

First, there was a *declaration.* When Philip asked the Ethiopian if he understood the Scripture passage he was reading, he responded, "How could I, unless someone guides me?" (v. 31). When I witnessed to a young man in Atlanta, he responded with a commitment to Christ. After making his commitment, he said to me, "I've been waiting five years for someone to help me get straightened out with God."

Paul's declaration to the Romans should challenge every Christian: "How then shall they call upon Him in whom they have not believed? And how shall they believe in Him whom they have not heard? And how shall they hear without a preacher? And how shall they preach unless they are sent?" (Rom. 10:14-15). The lost world needs a witness. Philip provided a witness for the Ethiopian which was based on Scripture and which focused on Jesus Christ (v. 35).

Second, there was a *decision.* The only way a person can be converted is to deliberately and personally believe in Jesus Christ. Exposure to a Christian witness is not enough. A person can't "catch" the

Christian faith. He or she must claim it through a personal decision. God has no grandchildren, only children. The Ethiopian made this decision because he told Philip, "I believe that Jesus Christ is the Son of God" (v. 37).

Third, there was a *demonstration*. One cannot be a secret disciple, for eventually the secrecy will destroy the discipleship, or the discipleship will destroy the secrecy. There are no private Christians, only individuals whose private decision is revealed in a public demonstration. The Ethiopian gave this demonstration. When he saw water, he asked Philip, "What prevents me from being baptized?" (v. 36). Then, Philip baptized him.

Fourth, there was another *declaration*. Converts become conveyors of the gospel so that others can become converts. This is God's plan, expressed clearly in 2 Timothy 2:2 which says: "The things which you have heard from me in the presence of many witnesses, these entrust to faithful men, who will be able to teach others also."

Tradition claims this Ethiopian went home and evangelized Ethiopia. That's why God called Philip from his effective ministry to many in the cities to go to the Gaza road where he talked to a single person (vv. 25-26). By leaving the cities, Philip reached a continent. By giving a witness to one, Philip became a part of an extended ministry to many.

What was the point of the Ethiopian incident? Luke wanted to show the power of God can change the life of non-Jews as well as Jews.

3. The Man

Philip was a man of *initiative.* When the angel gave him a command, "he arose and went" (v. 27). He didn't just sit back and wait. He went to the Gaza road, a much traveled road, where he would likely meet someone to whom he could speak. He went where the action was.

Philip was a man of *openness.* He went to Samaria where a "good" Jew would not go (v. 5). He went to a man of another race which a "good" Jew would not do (v. 30). He understood the universality of the gospel.

Philip was a man of *knowledge*. When he had the opportunity to witness to the Ethiopian, he started where the man was and from that point led him to Jesus (v. 35). He knew the Scripture well enough to explain it and apply it.

Philip was a man of *persuasiveness*. In Samaria, when Philip preached, the people listened to what he said, the possessed were liberated, the lame were lifted up, and there was great joy in the city (vv. 6-7). On the Gaza road, when Philip taught, the Ethiopian eunuch was saved and immediately wanted to be baptized (v. 38).

Philip was a man of *consistency*. He did not just stop with a few successes. Success did not lead to satisfaction but to a desire to share the gospel to others. Luke concluded the account of Philip with this statement: "As he passed through he kept preaching the gospel to all the cities" (v. 40). Philip is a model of consistency.

A Broadway legend tells of a playwright, cooped up in a telephone booth, holding the giant-sized New York telephone directory in his hands. He felt its great weight and looked curiously at its hundreds of pages of Joneses, Smiths, and Johnsons. Thinking in terms of his craft as a dramatist, the man exclaimed, "There's not much of a plot here, but man, what a cast." About today's church it can be said, "What a cast!" And what a plot there would be if deacons would emulate the pattern of Stephen and Philip.

7 Public Enemy Number One

Acts 9:1-31

John Henry Jowett, famous preacher of England, once said about Paul, "Every month I am more and more driven to Paul. I think you heard 'Paul' and 'Paul' and 'Paul' countless times in my ministry here. I think he has got the key. I feel that if ever mortal man had the key of the house I want opened he has got it."[1]

Paul was without question the pivotal figure in the church in the early days. F. F. Bruce said, "We cannot imagine the spread of Christianity in the Roman Empire apart from the work of Paul."[2]

In chapter 9, Luke focuses our attention for the first time on this missionary, church starter, preacher, author, and statesman of the early church.

Conversion (9:1-21)

No other event told about in Scripture, outside the story of Jesus Himself, is more important to the ongoing of God's kingdom than the conversion of Paul. The significance of the episode is seen in the fact that it is repeated two other times in full in the Book of Acts, in chapters 22 and 26. William Barclay calls it "the most famous conversion story in all history."[3] How are we to explain the experience of Paul described in our text?

Some try to explain the experience psychologically. They see it as "a strange hallucination" or a "psychological mystery." According to this view, Paul had an emotional catharsis from which he spun off in a new direction. It was also psychological.

Others explain the experience by means of natural phenomena.

The noise, they say, was not the voice of God but the crackling sound of an electrical storm commonly induced when the cold air from Mount Hermon met the hot breath of the desert. The light was not a glorious revelation of God's glory but the brilliance of the Damascan sun bearing down upon them at midday.

Still others explain the event physically. According to this view, Paul had an epileptic seizure from which he emerged a different man. Perhaps this physical dilemma of epilepsy was the oft-debated "thorn in the flesh" (2 Cor. 12:7).

Other explanations are offered. However, in the final analysis, only three alternatives are open to us. Either Paul invented the story as an excuse for his change of attitude toward Jesus, or he was deceived by a faulty interpretation of some natural phenomenon, or he has told what actually happened. Of the three, the last is fraught with less difficulties and seems to more fully explain the miraculous turn in Paul's life. What happened, simply stated, was that Paul came face-to-face with the living Christ.

Several things happened when Paul met Christ on the Damascus road.

1. Paul Put in Touch with God

When Paul met Christ, he was put in touch with God. The theological term for this is "reconciliation." *Reconciliation* is the bringing together of that which formerly was alienated and apart. As religious as Paul was in convictions, as righteous as he was in action, as rigorous as he was in determination, he was nevertheless at cross purposes with God. He and God were going in different directions. On the Damascus road they got together.

Only later could Paul articulate what had happened to him. For instance, in 2 Corinthians 5:19, he declared, "God was in Christ reconciling the world to himself." In Romans 5:10 he said, "While we were enemies, we were reconciled to God through the death of His Son." He was only able to describe that experience later. However, the experience that Paul articulated in all of the Epistles was the experience which happened on the Damascus road when Jesus took

Paul's hand and put it in the hand of God so that they could walk forward together.

2. Paul Changed into a New Person

When Paul met Christ and was put in touch with God, he was changed into a new person. The most evident fact of the story is that Paul's life was changed. He set off for Damascus as an apostle of the Sanhedrin, "breathing threats and murder against the disciples of the Lord" (Acts 9:1), with letters in hand that would authorize him to arrest Christians on the spot. He arrived in Damascus as an apostle of Christ, proclaiming in the synagogues that Jesus was the Son of God (Acts 9:20), with a desire in his heart to become part of the very Christian fellowship he had been persecuting. Paul who was the opponent of Christianity became the proponent of Christianity. He who hated Christ now heralded Christ. He who was going in one direction now was going in another direction. Paul's life was dramatically changed.

How beautifully Paul expressed this truth in 2 Corinthians 5:17: "Therefore if any man is in Christ, he is a new creature; the old things passed away; behold, new things have come." That was more than a theological explanation for Paul. It was a personal experience. Paul had a new allegiance, a new attitude, a new affection, and a new assignment. His life was changed.

At one revival meeting a young man felt the need to commit his life to Christ, and someone said to him, "Hold on. When I was saved, I really had to hold on."

Someone else said, "Let go. When I was saved, I really had to let go."

Yet another friend said, "Look for the light. When I was saved, I saw a light." Later, the man said that between holding on, letting go, and looking for the light, he almost missed being saved! Actually, no one form is normative for all Christians. What is normative is the result. Paul's life was changed on the Damascus road.

3. Paul Given the Holy Spirit

When Paul met Christ, was put in touch with God, and turned in a new direction, he was also given the Holy Spirit. Ananias explained to Paul that Christ came to him so that he could "be filled with the Holy Spirit" (9:17). The presence of the Holy Spirit in our lives is not something for which we have to strive or beg. He is not a special award given to the spiritually elite, nor a second blessing. He is a gift given to every Christian the moment we receive Jesus Christ as the Lord of our lives. The Holy Spirit comes with Jesus, and He comes to perform a unique ministry in our lives.

How can we describe the ministry of the Holy Spirit? The Holy Spirit is a *seal* who marks us off as belonging to God (Eph. 1:13). The Holy Spirit is a *sage* who teaches us the things of God (John 16:13). The Holy Spirit is a *sustainer* who provides the strength we will need to make it through each day (Rom. 8:11). The Holy Spirit is a *supplier* of spiritual gifts which we can use in carrying out the ministries of the church (1 Cor. 12:7). The Holy Spirit is a *supplicator* who steps in when we do not know how to pray as we should and "intercedes for us with groanings too deep for words" (Rom. 8:26). The Holy Spirit is a *substitute* for Christ, one just like Him, who will carry out in our lives the ministry Christ provided while He was on this earth (John 14:16). The Holy Spirit is a *sample* of the spiritual blessings that will be ours through all eternity (Eph. 1:14). The Holy Spirit is the indwelling presence of God in the life of every believer who supplies our every need, and when Paul met Christ, he was given the Holy Spirit.

4. Paul Identified with the Church

When Paul met Christ, he identified with God's people in the church. Notice three phrases which illustrate this. Luke said, "Immediately there fell from his eyes something like scales, and he regained his sight, and he arose and was baptized" (9:18). Luke added, "Now for several days he was with the disciples who were at Damascus" (9:19). Finally, Luke declared, "And when he had come to Jerusalem, he was trying to associate with the disciples" (9:26). Paul realized that commitment to Christ involved commitment to God's people.

Someone has said, "If religion does not begin with the individual, it does not begin; if it ends with the individual, it ends."[4] As a leg cannot live in isolation from the body, neither can a Christian live in isolation from the church. Therefore, we need to openly acknowledge our belongingness to the family of God like Paul by identifying with the church.

5. Paul Found What God Wanted Him to Do

When Paul met Christ, he found what God wanted him to do. Notice what the risen Christ said to Paul, "Rise, and enter the city, and it shall be told you what you must do" (9:6). Paul discovered three truths in this encounter.

First, Paul discovered Christ not only wanted to save him *from* something, but he also wanted to save him *for* something. How we need to make that discovery. We need to realize that as a Christian there are gifts that God has given us, and He expects us to use those gifts in performing a ministry for Him. We need to understand that God not only wants us to be something as a Christian, but He also wants us to do something. He has tasks He wants us to accomplish with our lives.

The greatest unemployment problem in the United States today is inside the church. People have the ability to teach, but are unemployed; people have administrative skills, but are unemployed; people have an ability to encourage and minister, but are unemployed; people possess God-given musical gifts, but are unemployed; and people are gifted to work with children and youth, but are unemployed.

In Paul's sermon in the synagogue at Pisidian Antioch he made an intriguing statement about David. He said, "For when David had served God's purpose in his own generation, he fell asleep" (Acts 13:36, NIV). He did not say that David was a great musician, a fearless warrior, a dynamic king, or a creative composer. He said David "served God's purpose." Life's highest honor is to find out what God wants us to do and then to do it.

Second, Paul discovered Christ's plan took priority over what he wanted to do. Before this encounter with the risen Christ, Paul did what he wanted to do, went where he wanted to go, and said what he wanted to say. From now on, Christ would call the shots of Paul's life.

As an eighteen-year-old, Jonathan Edwards wrote the following in his journal: "Resolved that all men should live to the glory of God. Resolved, secondly, that whether or not anyone else does, I will."[5] Paul realized God expects each of us to make that kind of commitment.

Third, Paul discovered the focal point of his ministry was the Gentiles. God said he was "to bear My name before the Gentiles (9:15).

An Englishman had a beautiful home on the coast. At one point, a huge rock jutted out into the sea. One day this man and his daughter stood on that summit and looked in every direction. The father decided to teach her a lesson about God. "Look up," he said, and she looked into the beautiful blue heaven. "Look down," he said, and she looked down at the waves crashing against the rocks below. He said, "Look out," and she looked out over the vast expanse of the sea. "Now, turn around and look out over the landscape," he said, and she saw the beauty of the land. Then he said, "Honey, so high, so deep, so wide, and so broad is the love of God."

After a moment, she said to her father, "If God's love is so high, so wide, so deep, and so broad, then we are living in the middle of it."[6]

In every age, some have tried to limit the love of God. Paul discovered there is no limit to God's love. God loved the Gentiles as well as the Jews. Because of God's love, Paul was commissioned to take the gospel to the Gentiles.

How would Paul discover these things? He would discover them through Ananias. Can you imagine how Ananias felt when God instructed him to go to Paul? Word had reached Damascus of Paul's intention. Most of the Damascan Christians, Ananias included, wanted to avoid Paul. They did not want Paul to find them because of their fear. God told Ananias to find the very man he did not want to see! To the credit of Ananias, his faith was stronger than his fear.

He responded to God's command with courage and with compassion. Ananias's courage motivated him to go to Paul (9:17). His compassion motivated him to address the former persecutor of the church with an address of affection: "Brother Saul" (9:17). Only the love of Christ can inspire that kind of compassion.

In a little mission church in New Zealand, a line of worshipers knelt at the altar rail to receive the Lord's Supper. Suddenly, from among them, a young native arose and returned to his pew. Some minutes later, he returned to his place at the rail. Afterwards, one of his friends asked what happened. The young man explained,

> When I went forward and knelt, I found myself side by side with a man whom some years ago had slain my father and whom I had vowed to kill. I couldn't partake of the Lord's Supper with him, so I returned to my pew. As I sat there, I thought about Jesus' statement at the first Lord's Supper: "By this all men will know that you are My disciples, if you have love for one another" (John 13:35). Then I looked up at the cross and saw Jesus hanging there and heard him say, "Father, forgive them; for they do not know what they are doing" (Luke 23:34). That's when I returned to the altar rail.[7]

Because of Christ's love for him, Ananias was able to love Paul. Enemies become brothers through the redeeming love of Christ. Through Ananias, Paul found out what Christ wanted him to do.

6. Paul Shared His Faith with Others

When Paul met Christ, he began to boldly share his faith with others. Luke said about Paul, "Immediately he began to proclaim Jesus in the synagogues, saying, 'He is the Son of God' " (Acts 9:20). These Jews in Damascus whom Paul wanted to enlist to persecute the followers of Christ were now being won to Christ by him. Paul realized witnessing is a natural consequence of an encounter with Christ. He also realized our witness needs to begin where we are with those who know us. The Jews of Damascus responded to Paul's witness with amazement.

If this encounter with Christ is all we have said it is, then we cannot keep from sharing it with others. Vance Havner described Christians as "God's post office." We are daily giving out messages of some sort to the world. These messages do not come from us, but they come through us. It is our responsibility to deliver these messages to the world. Havner added this challenging thought: "The tiniest post-office can bear a letter that may wreck or bless a nation." He concluded, "If you are a believer, you are God's postmaster in the little nook where you live. Keep the office clean, but do not make that more important than delivering the messages."[8]

Paul was by birth, a Jew; by citizenship, a Roman; and by education, a Greek. But by virtue of the encounter with Christ on the Damascus road, he was a Christian. And it was that encounter, not his birth, not his citizenship, not his education, which was the secret of Paul's life.

Communion

Between verses 21 and 22, we need to insert the experience of communion with God discussed in Galatians 1:15-17. Following Paul's conversion and preceding the culmination of Paul's ministry in Damascus, Paul went away to Arabia for three years.

What did Paul do in the Arabia? He spent time with God, fortifying his heart and clarifying his mind and consecrating his spirit to God's purpose for his life. These three years in Arabia are the key to Paul's spiritual power. He would face formidable foes throughout his ministry. Opponents and obstacles would constantly threaten him. In his own strength, Paul could not win. In the strength of God, Paul could not lose. Paul tapped God's strength in this three year sojourn in Arabia. In communion with God, Paul was empowered for the challenges ahead. After three years with God in the wilderness, Paul returned to Damascus.

Conflict (9:22-30)

Paul immediately had to call on the spiritual resource he built in his wilderness sojourn. After Paul's dramatic conversion, one would expect celebration. Instead, the result was conflict. Paul's situation was not unlike the man, during the Civil War, who wanted to be neutral.

He wore Yankee pants and a Confederate shirt. When he went out, both sides shot at him! Both sides shot at Paul; the Jews were angry about his conversion to Christianity, and the Christians were suspicious of it.

1. From Without (9:23-25)

Conflict was directed at Paul from without. Jews, perhaps some of his former friends, were aware of how damaging Paul could be in their attempts to destroy this new faith centered in Jesus Christ. He was a living testimony of the power of Jesus to change lives. Therefore, he needed to be removed from the scene. An attempt to kill Paul was thwarted by Paul's Christian friends, who facilitated his escape in a large basket that they lowered through a hole in the wall.

2. From Within (9:26-27)

Surprisingly, conflict also came from within. Luke said, "When he had come to Jerusalem, he was trying to associate with the disciples; and they were all afraid of him, not believing that he was a disciple" (9:26). Fear was so great that Paul's witness for the church might have been lost had it not been for "Mr. Encourager." Barnabas lived up to his nickname by standing up for Paul and bringing support for him in the church. Consequently, Paul was able to preach with liberty and boldness (9:28).

Culmination (9:31)

In the aftermath of Paul's conversion, the church enjoyed a time of peace and prosperity. Several factors contributed to this time of relief. With the conversion of Paul, no real leader gave impetus to the persecution. On the positive side, the results of Paul's preaching were felt not just in Judea, but in Galilee and Samaria as well. Secular historians reveal another helpful occurrence for the church. About this time, the emperor Caligula attempted to force the Jews to worship him as God. Thus, the attention of the Jerusalem authorities was distracted from the new Christian sect to the more pressing problem of Caligula. As a result of this breathing spell, the church experienced two things.

1. Harmony

Luke says the churches "enjoyed peace, being built up" (9:31). The period of persecution had driven the Christians closer together. In addition, the story of Paul's conversion increased the confidence of the Christians, thus strengthening the fellowship of the church.

2. Growth

The lack of pressure outside the church and the increase of confidence inside the church resulted in numerical growth. Inward progress ("being built up") led to outward progress ("continued to increase"). More than human forces were at work, however. Luke explained this growth came about because of "the comfort of the Holy Spirit" (9:31). This equation reappears throughout the Book of Acts: boldness $+$ witness $+$ the power of the Holy Spirit $=$ growth.

The curtain falls on the first act of Paul's ministry. Continued rejection of his message by the Jews and their plots to kill him provided the impetus for Paul to leave Jerusalem. He returned to his home town of Tarsus (9:30), where he would develop a home base for his ministry. From there, Paul ministered in "the regions of Syria and Cilicia" (Gal. 1:21). We do not hear of him again until Acts 11:25, seven years later, when Barnabas enlisted his assistance to minister at Antioch.

8 | The Making of a Rock

Acts 9:32—11:18; 12:1-24

It is difficult to follow the chronology in the Book of Acts from chapter 8 to chapter 13, and there is a reason for this confusion. This is a transition section as Luke moved from an emphasis on Peter to an emphasis on Paul. Luke brought to a close the story of Peter and the significant part he played in the early Christian movement. He began the next great development of the church, the movement of the gospel to the Gentiles, in which Paul became the leading character.

The last we saw of Peter was in Acts 8:25. He was returning to Jerusalem after a scouting expedition to the Samaritans. Peter evidently began an itinerant ministry among the dispersed Christian communities of Judea.

His Power (9:32-43)

Simon Peter was beginning to fade into the background in Luke's unfolding story of the church. However, Luke made sure that when Peter faded, he faded in a blaze of glory. Luke focused on the healing power of Jesus Christ which was channeled through Simon Peter.

1. The Healing of Aeneas (9:33-35)

Peter carried out a ministry of teaching and healing in the city of Lydda. Luke discussed one of the incidents in Lydda—the healing of Aeneas. We see once more that Peter was a man of energy and enterprise. He saw a need, and he was compelled to meet that need. In Lydda, a city about 25 miles from Jerusalem, Peter met a man named Aeneas. Aeneas had been immobilized for eight years by some kind of paralysis. Like he did for the lame man who cried out for help in Acts 3, Peter healed Aeneas. Immediately, the man was able to get out of bed and walk. Notice the emphasis on the source and result of this miracle of healing.

What was the *source* of this miracle of healing? The emphasis was not on Peter but on Jesus. Peter did not say to this paralytic, "I heal you." Instead, he said, "Jesus Christ heals you" (9:34). The healing power did not come from Peter. Rather, it came through Peter. Jesus was the Source.

What was the *result* of this miracle of healing? Luke said, "All who lived at Lydda and Sharon saw him, and they turned to the Lord" (9:35). Because Peter pointed to Jesus as the Source of the healing, the healing itself pointed people to Jesus.

2. The Healing of Dorcas (9:36-43)

Peter also carried out a ministry of teaching and healing in the city of Joppa. Joppa was the city from which Jonah tried to escape God's challenge to preach the gospel to the Gentiles. Ironically, Peter went to that same city in order to preach the gospel to the Gentiles. Out of Peter's productive ministry in Joppa, Luke discussed one incident. In the city of Joppa was a woman believer named Tabitha. Dorcas was her Greek name. The word means "gazelle" and speaks of the gracefulness and gentleness of her spirit. We see several things about Dorcas.

First, Dorcas *believed something.* She is called a disciple (9:36). Dorcas was a woman who believed in Jesus as her Lord. The secret of Dorcas's life was that she believed Jesus was who He claimed to be— God's Son, humanity's Savior, the Lord of life, the hope of history.

Second, Dorcas *felt something.* The widows weeping at her death bed were reacting to the loss of someone from whom they had felt love, understanding, and empathy. Dorcas was a woman who not only had a committed mind, but she also had a compassionate heart.

Third, Dorcas *did something.* As the widows gathered around her death bed, they not only had the remembrance of her love in their hearts but also had on their bodies the very coats and tunics she had made for them. Dorcas made the magnificent move from the passive to the active. She translated good intentions and sympathetic feelings into tangible actions.

Because of the power of Jesus channeled through Peter's life, Dorcas was restored to her life of compassion and service. Notice again the power for the healing was from God. Before Peter healed Dorcas, he prayed (9:40). Not only did the power in Peter's life come from Jesus, but also the manifestation of that power pointed people to Jesus. After the healing of Dorcas, Luke said, "It became known all over Joppa, and many believed in the Lord" (9:42).

His Perception (10:1—11:18)

The Book of Acts is the exciting story of the spread of Christianity from its provincial beginning to a place of worldwide prominence. Luke told the story of the dramatic expansion of Christianity from Jerusalem to Judea, to Samaria, and then to the ends of the earth. As the gospel spread, one barrier after another was broken down. One of those momentous barriers or breaking experiences—occurred in the experience of Cornelius.

Of all the barriers in the ancient world perhaps the barrier between the Jew and the Gentile was the most formidable. The Jews and the Gentiles were worlds apart in their thinking, completely segregated in their activity. Yet in this story we see the barrier broken down as Gentiles became a part of the Christian church along with the Jews.

The importance of this story is shown by the minute details Luke recorded and by the repetition of the story in chapter 11. This was Luke's way of saying, "This is a significant happening in the early church, a key event which determined the ultimate direction Christianity would take." The key to the story is the changing perception of Peter.

1. The Person (10:1-8)

The person around whom the story revolves was a man named Cornelius. What a profile of him we are given. Cornelius was a man of *courage*. Luke said Cornelius was "a centurion of what was called the Italian cohort" (10:1).

The city of Caesarea was the headquarters for the procurator of Judea, Samaria, and Idumea. In the city was an Italian cohort which consisted of about six hundred seasoned soldiers. They were stationed there for the purpose of protecting the procurator and keeping order. The cohort was divided into groups of one hundred. Over each one hundred men was a noncommissioned officer called a centurion. The centurions were held in high esteem in the ancient world. One historian said, "Centurions are required not to be bold and adventurous so much as good leaders of steady and prudent mind, not prone to take the offensive or start fighting wantonly, but able when overwhelmed and hard pressed to stand fast and die at their post."[1] Cornelius, as a centurion, was a man of great courage.

Cornelius was also a man of *character*. The Bible calls him "a devout man, and one who feared God" (10:2). The term *God-fearer* was more than just a description. This label was given to those non-Jews in the ancient world who were attracted to the Jewish belief in one God and to the high ethical standards of Jewish religion. These God-fearers did not actually become converts to Judaism, but they devoted themselves to the study of the law and followed the worship patterns and moral standards of the Jews. Cornelius was thus a man of integrity and ethical uprightness. He was a man of character.

Cornelius was a man of *charity*. Luke said Cornelius "gave many alms to the Jewish people" (10:2).

Lord Shaftesbury of England, on one occasion, was going to meet some people in a city where he had never been. They did not know him and were afraid they would not recognize him when he got off the train, so they asked his secretary to describe him. She said, "Look for a tall man getting off the train helping someone—that will be Lord Shaftesbury." That could be said about Cornelius. He was always helping others through his gifts of love. He was a man of charity.

Cornelius was a man of *communion*. Luke said Cornelius "prayed to God continually" (10:2). He was a man whose life was permeated with prayer. E. Stanley Jones once said, "I find myself better or worse as I pray more or less. It works with almost mathematical precision."[2] Like E. Stanley Jones, Cornelius was a man of communion.

When we see this profile of the man, we see that Cornelius was a beautiful example of high moral living. He was an ideal citizen, a courageous leader, religious person, and moral man. He was as fine as a man could be. The point of the story, however, was that his courage, character, charity, and communion were not enough to make him a Christian. As good as Cornelius was, he was not good enough. Something more was needed. He needed Jesus.

2. The Preparation (10:9-33)

Before Peter, a Jew, could communicate with Cornelius, a Gentile, God had to do some preparation. God prepared Simon Peter to speak (10:9-13). In a vision, repeated three times, God taught Peter that no person was to be considered unclean or unacceptable. Because of the vision, Peter was able to do two things that a Jew would never do: allow a Gentile to enter his home for the purpose of table fellowship (10:23) and go into a Gentile home for table fellowship (10:26). God prepared Peter for the task He wanted him to do.

God also prepared Cornelius to listen (10:30-33). Cornelius, too, had a vision from God. His vision was not of a sheet filled with animals, but of a man in bright clothing who instructed him to call for Peter and listen to what he had to say. The culmination of the process of preparation is found in verse 33 where Cornelius said, "Now then, we are all here present before God to hear all that you have been commanded by the Lord."

God is still preparing people to hear and receive the gospel today. We may never talk to a person in whose life God has not already done some of this preparatory work. God does this preparatory work through the Holy Spirit. At the present time, this preparatory work is being done in a more extensive way than ever before in our history. People today are hungry for a genuine spiritual experience. People are hurting for a word of hope and comfort. People are hunting for a purpose to live. As it was with Cornelius, so it is with the multitudes in our day; many are ready to get serious about God.

3. The Proclamation (10:34-43)

Never has a preacher had a more attentive audience than did Simon Peter that day at Caesarea. Notice the message Peter proclaimed.

Peter presented Jesus as the *peace of God*. Peter said, "The word which He sent to the sons of Israel, preaching peace through Jesus Christ" (10:36). Humanity is estranged from God. Jesus is the One who brings us back together and restores peace between us.

Peter presented Jesus as the *power of God*. Peter declared about Jesus, "God anointed Him with the Holy Spirit and with power" (10:38). Humans need more than peace with God. They need power to live out their lives. That power is available in Christ Jesus.

He presented Jesus as the *presence of God*. Peter explained the special presence of God in Jesus' life when he declared, "God was with Him" (10:38). Jesus was more than a messenger from God. He was more than a prophet of God. He was God Himself, incarnate in human flesh, and dwelling among men.

Peter presented Jesus as the *pardon of God*. Peter said, "Through His name everyone who believes in Him receives forgiveness of sins" (10:43). For all of his goodness and in his moments of clearest insight, Cornelius was aware of the dark shadow of sin in his life. He knew he needed to be forgiven. He needed to be pardoned from his past. That forgiveness was made possible through Jesus Christ.

Someone gave this suggestion to preachers: know your stuff, know who you're stuffing, and then stuff them. This is just what Simon Peter did. He sensed Cornelius' estrangement, so he presented Jesus as the peace of God. He discerned Cornelius' feeling of inadequacy, so he presented Jesus as the power of God. Peter felt Cornelius' sense of aloneness, so he presented Jesus as the presence of God. He saw Cornelius' guilt, so he presented Jesus as the pardon of God. Simon Peter presented Christ, and in the midst of his message, Cornelius yielded his life. In that moment of acceptance, Cornelius was ushered into the family of God.

4. The Proof (10:44-48)

That the gospel was for the Gentiles, as well as for the Jews, was a fact that would not be easily accepted among the Jewish Christians. Some dramatic, undeniable sign from God was needed to confirm this fact. God's stamp of approval on this monumental step was needed. God gave such a sign. While Peter was still preaching, in the middle of his message, before the laying on of hands, and before the baptism, the Holy Spirit descended on all the Gentiles who heard and believed. These new Gentile believers "were speaking with tongues and exalting God" (10:46).

These manifestations of the Spirit were a sign given at a particular time for a particular reason. They were given to establish once and for all that the gospel of Jesus Christ would not be limited by any racial barriers. It was available to all people of all races and all nations. The special manifestation of the Holy Spirit was proof that Cornelius and those with him had, indeed, become Christians.

5. The Principle

Peter proclaimed, "I most certainly understand now that God is not one to show partiality, but in every nation the man who fears Him and does what is right, is welcome to Him" (10:34-35). God is no "respecter" of persons. He is not one to show partiality. His kingdom is for everyone. That is the principle this story proclaims, and we see this principle in action all through the New Testament.

In the Demoniac at Gadara, Jesus reached a troubled man (Mark 5). In Nicodemus, Jesus reached a man who seemed to have it all together (John 3). In Zacchaeus, Jesus reached a wealthy man (Luke 19). In the lame beggar at the temple healed by Peter and John, Jesus reached a poor man (Acts 3). In Simon Peter, Jesus reached a Jewish man (John 1). In Luke, Jesus reached a Gentile man (Col. 4:14). In John Mark, Jesus reached a young man (Acts 12:25). In Simeon at the temple, when Jesus was dedicated, Jesus reached an old man (Luke 2:25). In blind Bartimaeus, Jesus reached a man of insignificance (Mark 10). In Cornelius, He reached a man of authority (Acts 10).

God is no respecter of persons, but in every nation of every social class and in every economic group of every race, the one who fears God is welcome to Him. It may be said about the family of God, no one is so good he or she should stay out, and no one is so bad he or she cannot enter in.

6. The Presentation (11:1-18)

The key issue was this: Is Christianity just for the Jews, or is it for everyone? Knowing the Spirit of Jesus, it is difficult to understand why that was an issue, but inborn prejudices are hard to shake. A Jewish element, identified as the "circumcised" believers (11:2), criticized Peter for allowing Gentiles to become Christians. Peter retold the story of his experience with Cornelius, climaxing with the statement: "If God therefore gave to them the same gift as He gave to us also after believing in the Lord Jesus Christ, who was I that I could stand in God's way?" (11:17). That settled the issue for the moment (11:18).

Why was this such an important issue? It was a significant issue because the fate of Christianity was at stake. If the more Jewish element had won the day, Christianity would have been locked within the limits of Judaism. The very spirit of Christianity would have been quenched.

It was a significant issue because the following of Peter was at stake. Until now, Peter's word was the final authority. With this issue, Peter moved on the defensive. James, who aligned himself more strictly with the Jewish element, assumed leadership in the church. Peter's influence began to fade.

Although the issue was settled formally, many of the Jewish Christians remained adamant in their position. This is confirmed in the next verse. Luke said the ones who were scattered limited their preaching to Jews only. The debate about the requirements for salvation between the Jews and Gentiles would lead eventually to the first council of the church described in Acts 15.

His Persecution (12:1-24)

Who was this Herod we read about in verse 1, and why did he lay hands on some who belonged to the church in order to do them harm? He was Herod Agrippa I, who ruled over Judea from A.D. 41-44. He was the grandson of Herod the Great, who ruled at the time Jesus was born.

Luke gave us an insight into the motivation of Herod. Luke said Herod did what he did to please the Jews. That's why he arrested James and put him to death. That's why he arrested Peter and planned to do the same to him. That's why Herod initiated this new wave of persecution, because the persecution of the Christians enhanced his popularity with his Jewish constituents. Herod was playing the game of power politics. The Christians were merely convenient pawns he moved around to strengthen his hand.

However, Luke included this incident about Peter not to inform us of Herod Agrippa, but to describe how these first Christians made it through one of their darkest hours. The faith of the first Christians was still alive. Yet, their faith was challenged from two different directions. Peter was the central character in the drama.

1. Faith Tested from Without (12:1-11)

Up to this point, the church was doing well. The earlier wave of persecution initiated by the religious leaders in Jerusalem, instead of destroying the faith, had actually been an impetus to growth and expansion. These early Christians had what modern-day sports commentators call momentum. In Acts 12, the momentum suddenly swings against them. With James dead, Peter in jail, and their backs against the wall, all the military might of Rome was behind this local ruler who seemed bent and determined to abolish these people called Christians. What a challenge to their faith this experience was. Our faith today is also challenged from the outside. As for them, so for us, when we seek to live the Christian life, when we assert our faith in Christ, we are confronted by pressures from without which challenge our faith.

Sometimes our faith is challenged by *outside problems*. Paul cataloged these problems in 2 Corinthians 4:8-9 when he wrote, "We are afflicted in every way, but not crushed; perplexed, but not despairing; persecuted, but not forsaken; struck down, but not destroyed." Paul mentioned afflictions, the normal irritations of life that everybody faces; perplexities, the experiences in life that leave us baffled as to what to do; persecutions, a word which covers a range of negative reactions directed toward the Christian; and catastrophes, those traumatic experiences which try our faith to the limit. As it was in Paul's day, so it is in ours, our faith is often challenged by outside problems.

Our faith is also challenged by *outside powers*. This is where faith was tested for these early Christians and where many of our Christian brothers in other countries feel the challenge to their faith today. The power of the government can often be an enemy of faith. Even more awesome is the power of Satan, prowling around like a "roaring lion, seeking someone to devour" (1 Pet. 5:8). The New Testament reminds us that our battle is not against flesh and blood but against principalities and powers.

Our faith is also challenged by *outside people*. Throughout the biblical story, God's leaders had to deal with individuals who opposed them. For Moses, there was Pharaoh. For David, there was King Saul. For Elijah, there was Jezebel. Many times, we today have individuals who are self-appointed committees dedicated to the purpose of making life miserable for us.

Whether it is from outside problems, outside powers, or outside people, every one of us will have our faith challenged from without. Notice two ingredients with which these early Christians confronted this outside challenge—the prayer of the people and the power of God. "Peter was kept in the prison," Acts tells us, "but prayer for him was being made fervently by the church of God" (12:5). That was the key which unlocked the door of that jail and set Peter free. Likewise, that is the key which will enable us to stand fast in the midst of the heaviest burden life can dump on our shoulders. That is the key which will enable us to win victory over the principalities and powers of this world. That is the key which will enable us to resist the antagonism of those who stand against us. The power of God and the prayer of His people that releases that power are the keys to victory over the challenges to faith from without.

2. Faith Tested from Within (12:12-24)

The greatest challenge to the faith of these first Christians was not from without but from within. Don't miss the humorous side of their ironic reaction to Peter's release. Realizing he was free and knowing that all the Christians were gathered at Mary's house praying for his release, Peter went immediately to tell them. When Rhoda saw Peter she was so shocked she forgot to let him in (12:14). Then when she told the others they responded, "[Rhoda,] you are out of your mind!" It couldn't be Simon Peter! (12:15).

Do you see what they were saying? They were saying, "Don't interrupt us with news of Peter's release from prison because we are too busy praying for his release. Don't bother us with word of a miracle from God because we are too busy praying for a miracle from God." Why would they react like that? Because their faith was too small. They were going through the motions, but they didn't really expect something to happen.

Do you remember when Jesus returned to Nazareth, His hometown, to share God's good news? Already He had brought sight to the blind, but no blind eyes were opened in Nazareth. Already He had loosed the tongue of a man enabling him to speak, but no immobile tongues were liberated in Nazareth. Already the sick and lame had been healed by the Great Physician, but no healings were done by Jesus in Nazareth. Already He had performed mighty miracles, but no miracles were performed in Nazareth.

Why? Why was the power of God which had been so available, not experienced in Nazareth? The Gospel writer told us: "He did not do many miracles there because of their unbelief" (Matt. 13:58). They did not expect anything to happen. Therefore, it didn't.

The greatest challenge to faith today, the greatest hindrance to God's work today, is not from without but from within. It is not from the principalities and powers of this world or the problems of daily life or the people around us who don't believe. Our challenge comes from within, from the lack of vision, the satisfaction with mediocrity, the comfort of the status quo, the absence of the spirit of adventure, and the refusal to take risks which exists in the lives of God's people.

Carl Bates spoke of a time in his life when he earnestly prayed, "God, I want your power." Time passed, and the power did not come. So he prayed again with a real burden, "God, why haven't you answered that prayer?"

God answered with this simple reply, "With plans no bigger than yours, you don't need my power."

How big are our plans? Since our plans are determined by our vision, and our vision by our faith, let me rephrase the question: "How big is our faith?" Is it big enough to move out of the patterns in which we have been comfortably settled and break some new ground for God? Is it big enough to lead us to make plans for our churches which are so far reaching that they cannot possibly be accomplished apart from the power of God?

Somewhere I heard a man say, "I spent twenty years trying to come to terms with my doubts. Then one day it dawned on me that I had better come to terms with my faith. Now I have passed from the agony of questions I cannot answer into the agony of answers I cannot escape."

These early Christians, led by Peter, finally came to terms with their faith. Inspired by the agony of answers they could not escape, they were ready to win the world for Jesus Christ.

9 | The Vision Expands

Acts 11:19-30; 12:25—14:28

In the thirteenth chapter of Acts, we come to a point of transition in the book. Beginning in this chapter, we see three changes.

First, we see a change of *person*. Luke moved from an emphasis on Peter to an emphasis on Paul. In chapter 15, there is one last glimpse of Peter, but from that point on Paul is in center stage.

We see a change of *proclamation*. Luke moved from an emphasis on the Jews to an emphasis on the Gentiles. For the very first time, the gospel is deliberately, purposefully preached to the Gentiles. That pattern is followed throughout the remainder of the book.

We also see a change of *place*. Luke moved from an emphasis on Jerusalem to an emphasis on Antioch. Except for chapter 15, the church at Antioch now held center stage.

The Church (11:19-30)

This city of Antioch, which was the center of the new wave of Christian mission, was the capital of the province of Syria, guarded by a garrison of four legions. It was the third largest city in the Roman Empire with a population of about 500,000. The city was pervaded by immorality. This immorality was not condemned by the established religion but rather was condoned by it. "The city was proverbial for its lax sexual morals; this reputation was mainly due to the cult of Artemis and Appollo at Daphne, five miles distant, where the ancient Syrian worship of Astarte, with its ritual prostitution, was carried on under Greek nomenclature."[1] Antioch was an important city politically, economically, and religiously. In the city of Antioch, God planted a church that was to hold center stage for the remainder of the Book of Acts. What kind of church was it?

1. Evangelistic in Nature

The Christians in Antioch focused on sharing their faith. They witnessed to the Jews (11:19). They also extended their witness to the Gentiles (11:20). Their witness brought tremendous results: "The hand of the Lord was with them, and a large number who believed turned to the Lord" (11:21). This church understood that its primary purpose was to share the message about Jesus Christ with others. They were evangelistic in nature.

Studies have been done on growing churches and why they grow. Of all the different factors cited, one is almost always present. Growing churches major on direct evangelism. Growing churches have mobilized and trained their lay people to share their faith.

Two basic kinds of evangelism are effective: attraction evangelism and proclamation evangelism. Attraction evangelism happens when a person lives such a Christlike life that others are influenced to come to Christ by the way he or she lives. Proclamation evangelism happens when a person gives a verbal witness, and others are influenced to come to Christ by what he or she says. Which is the most important? Both are important. In fact, the most effective evangelism is when the two coincide. One man, who came forward to make a decision for Christ, said to the pastor, "I watched how you lived. I listened to you preach. And I noticed that the two matched up."

That kind of evangelism is the key ingredient of growing churches. A church occupying center stage in God's kingdom work is a church like the one at Antioch which was evangelistic in nature.

2. Sound in Doctrine

After the Antioch church began to grow, the Jerusalem church sent Barnabas to investigate. When he saw what was happening, he stayed to instruct. He, in turn, brought Paul to help him. Together they developed the new Christians into disciples. Luke said, "It came about that for an entire year they met with the church and taught considerable numbers" (11:26). The church at Antioch understood its purpose was not only to register decisions but also to make disciples. They were not only involved in evangelism but also in edification, building up the believers in the faith.

W. E. Sangster, outstanding Methodist preacher of the past, often expressed concern over the spiritual ignorance of today's Christian. He traced the problem back to the pulpit and concluded, "All the evidence goes to show that a great deal of Protestant preaching for a generation past has been on marginal things." We have been "toying with trifles" and "ensnared by novelty," he said, instead of feeding our people on the strong meat of God's Word.[2]

One woman said to her pastor as she left the worship service, "Pastor, it is so nice to come hear you preach and not have to think about anything." That is not nice; that is tragic. The result is churches full of Christians who are so shallow in their understanding of the faith that they fall prey to every new idea and novel teaching that comes along.

A church occupying center stage in God's kingdom work is a church like the one at Antioch which, through strong doctrinal preaching and perseverance in personal study and involvement in small discipleship groups, is sound in doctrine. Each member has the responsibility to be a mature Christian.

3. Bold in Character

Luke made an unusual statement about these first Christians: "The disciples were first called Christians in Antioch" (11:26). The suffix "ian" was added to the word *Christ* as a label for these believers in Antioch. That suffix means "belonging to the party of" or "transacting business in the name of." The Antioch church exhibited such a Christlikeness in character that they were easily recognized as those who belonged to the party of Christ.

This is remarkable when we remember the kind of city Antioch was. Antioch was known far and wide for its luxurious immorality. The chariot races, the gambling, and the deliberate pursuit of pleasure went on day and night in Antioch. "The morals of Daphne," said William Barclay, "was a phrase that all the world knew for loose and lustful living."[3] In that kind of city, surrounded by that kind of immorality, these Christians lived with such boldness of character that they could be easily identified as Christ-ones.

To claim we cannot live a moral life in our immoral world today or to declare that the pressure of the crowd is so great we can no longer live by the standards of the Bible is a cop-out. Our world today is no better nor worse than was the city of Antioch.

A church occupying center stage in God's kingdom work is a church like the one at Antioch which was bold in character.

4. Caring in Attitude

Luke told of a prophet who came to Antioch and predicted a great famine that would especially affect Judea (11:27). What did the Christians of Antioch do? How did they respond? Each of the Christians, according to his or her income, pledged an amount of money for a relief fund to be sent to Judea. The church at Antioch recognized the fact that they were a part of one big family and, as brothers and sisters, they could be open in expressing their needs and caring in meeting those needs.

We wear so many masks in the church. We have so many hidden hurts we are afraid to admit. We have so many problems we are afraid to share with each other. I long for the day when we will experience the kind of love in the church that will free us to honestly admit our struggles and our failures and our hurts to each other so that we can begin to, "Bear one another's burdens, and thus fulfill the law of Christ" (Gal. 6:2). Cecil Osborne gave this definition of the church: "A gathering place for all who were hurt and wanted relief and all who were compassionate and wanted to help."[4] What a beautiful description of the church!

A church occupying center stage in God's kingdom work is a church like the one at Antioch which was caring in attitude.

5. Cooperative in Spirit

When Barnabas saw all that was happening in Antioch, he realized he could not handle the situation alone, so he went to Tarsus and brought Paul to Antioch. He was not concerned about being the head person. He was not concerned about who received the credit. His only concern was that the work of God would be done. He worked cooperatively so that together, these Christians could do what alone they could not do. The key to the church at Antioch was the cooperative spirit with which they worked.

The Commissioning (12:25—13:5)

"Familiarity breeds contempt" is a well-worn phrase we all understand. This phrase refers to our tendency to take for granted, even to despise, that to which we are continuously exposed. Nowhere is that tendency more likely to appear than when we approach the section of Acts that describes "the missionary journeys of Paul." Those of us who have grown up in the church have been fed repeated doses of Paul's missionary adventures as long as we can remember. Still, I am convinced there is more light yet to break forth from God's Word. In this familiar passage, we have some pivotal insights into the nature of the church's mission.

A study of the New Testament will reveal three dimensions of the church's mission. The New Testament describes the upward dimension that has to do with our relationship to God. The New Testament also describes the inward dimension that has to do with our relationship with each other in the church. In addition, the New Testament refers to an outward dimension that has to do with our relationship with those who are outside the church. The outward dimension is the focus in this section of Acts. What can we say about this outward mission of the church?

1. Primary

The Holy Spirit said to the Christians at Antioch, "Set apart for Me Barnabas and Saul for the work to which I have called them" (13:2). From the beginning, this has been the work to which the church has been called, to take the gospel to the world. We find the command in all four of the Gospels. "Go into all the world and preach the gospel to all creation" is the way this challenge is expressed in the last verses of Mark's Gospel (16:15). "Go therefore and make disciples of all the nations" is the way Matthew put the challenge (28:19). Luke's Gospel ends with the declaration of the risen Lord "that repentance for forgiveness of sins should be proclaimed in His name to all the nations" (24:47). John's version of the mission of the church is found in Jesus' high priestly prayer for His disciples, "As Thou didst send Me into the world, I also have sent them into the world" (17:18).

The real test of orthodoxy in the church is obedience to the command of Jesus and in all four Gospels, Jesus declared this to be the mission of the church: "Go into all the world" with the gospel. Emil Brunner wrote, "The church exists by mission, just as a fire exists by burning. Where there is no mission, there is no church; and where there is neither church nor mission, there is no faith."[5]

A church not concerned about missions or a Christian not involved in missions ignores the one major task for which Christ left us in this world. The call to missions is primary.

2. Personal

The Holy Spirit gave specific instructions, "Set apart for me Barnabas and Saul" (Acts 13:2). The good news of God is not proclaimed to the world by angels, delivered from heaven by impersonal voices, or dropped out of the sky in leaflets. In each generation, the gospel is delivered by living, breathing men and women who speak from their own experiences. People like Paul and Barnabas in every age have been set aside by the Holy Spirit for this purpose. The mission of the church is personal.

Picture this scene on a football field. One team, which averages about 120 pounds per man, is lined up on offense against another team on which each man weighs over 190 pounds. The coach has called the first play for Johnson, who is the fullback, to take the ball off tackle. Instead, the quarterback fakes a handoff to Johnson and tries a bootleg around the end. He is smothered! The coach sends in a player who tells the quarterback to give the ball to Johnson. This time the quarterback fakes a handoff to Johnson, then gives the ball to the halfback who goes straight into the line and is creamed. This time, the coach yells from the sideline, "I said, 'Give the ball to Johnson!' " On the field, Johnson steps back from the huddle and yells to the coach, "Johnson doesn't want the ball!" That is the tragedy of the modern church; Christians whom the Holy Spirit wants to set aside for the work to which they have been called yell out to God, "Johnson doesn't want the ball!"

The mission of the church will be accomplished in the world when individuals like you and me decide to become involved. Missions is personal.

3. Prophetic

Luke gave this early report on the first missionaries: "When they reached Salamis, they began to proclaim the word of God in the synagogues of the Jews" (13:5). Missions involves the prophetic declaration of the Word of God.

John R. W. Stott shared an important insight when he said evangelism, the mission to which we have been called, is not to be defined in terms of its results. In the New Testament, evangelism does not mean to win converts. Evangelism means to announce the good news, regardless of the results.[6] That insight is comforting, because it reminds us we are not responsible to convert anyone, nor are we able to. We are not responsible to save anyone, nor are we able to. The result is our preaching depends not on us but on God. Personal witnessing results depend not on us but on God. We are responsible simply to proclaim the Word, to plant the seeds, and then to pray for the harvest.

This is the primary work which each of us, as Christians, has been called to do: to present to the world the good news of God's love as it was revealed to us in Jesus Christ. We are to do this through what we say (proclamation), through what we are (witness), and through what we do (service). We are simply to plant the seeds and trust God for the harvest.

The Conflict (13:6-13)

As Paul and Barnabas proclaimed the gospel, they were immediately confronted by opposition (13:6-8). A false prophet named Bar-Jesus (or Elymas, as he is called in v. 8), opposed Paul, seeking to turn the proconsul away from the faith. Whenever the gospel is preached or the demand for discipleship begins to threaten the personal interests of people, some are going to react and sometimes violently.

How timid we have become in our day. At the first sign of trouble, we pull back the forces. The least bit of opposition can stop us in our tracks. The least bit of criticism silences us. We look around and see the obstacles standing in the way of reaching modern humanity with the message of Christ, so we don't even try. The truth is that problems and obstacles have always been common companions to the mission enterprise of the church.

The Jews began to contradict Paul and arouse opposition to him (13:45). Did Paul quit? No. Rather, the next verse tells us: "Paul and Barnabas spoke out boldly."

Opposition was so great in Antioch of Pisidia that Paul and Barnabas were driven out of that district (13:50). Did Paul and Barnabas give up? No. They went straight to Iconium, entered the synagogue, and spoke in such a manner that a great multitude believed (14:1).

Luke said, "But the Jews who disbelieved stirred up the minds of the Gentiles, and embittered them against the brethren" (14:2). Did Paul get discouraged? No. Luke added, "Therefore, they spent a long time there speaking boldly with reliance upon the Lord" (14:3).

Luke told of the stoning of Paul (14:19). The people of the city of Lystra stoned Paul, dragged him out of the city, and left him for dead. Was this the end of Paul's mission? No, because Paul rose up, went to Derbe, and preached the gospel in that city.

The way Paul knew whether he had a good Sunday was to count his bandages on Monday. Opposition did not stop him. Persecution did not dissuade him. Problems did not discourage him. Paul was on a mission for God, and he would not be stopped.

As we carry out our missions, we, like Paul, will be opposed by criticism and mocked by people. We will be tempted to quit by those who say our work is not important. Every church and every Christian must decide to listen to the voice of God rather than to the voice of others. When we do that, we will hear God's command to proclaim the whole gospel for the whole person to the whole world.

When conflict comes, we can respond in one of two ways.

1. We Can Go Forward

In the midst of the problems Paul faced (13:6-8), he was nevertheless able to experience victory because he persisted in his proclamation. Luke said, "Then the proconsul believed when he saw what had happened, being amazed at the teaching of the Lord" (13:12).

We are not responsible for the results, but when we proclaim God's Word and plant the seed, we have this promise: God's Word will not return void. The prophet Isaiah said,

So shall my word be that goes forth from my mouth;
it shall not return to me empty,
but it shall accomplish that which I purpose,
and prosper in the thing for which I sent it (55:11, RSV).

People can be reached. Lives can be changed. The lost can be saved if we will be faithful to our mission and if we will go forward.

2. We Can Go Home

Luke told us that young Mark decided he would rather go home than go forward, so he left the mission expedition. Why did Mark quit? Perhaps Mark quit because of the *situation*. When he thought about the unknown land toward which he, Paul, and Barnabas were headed, the hard ground upon which they would sleep, and the gangs of robbers hiding in the narrow mountain passes, he went home because he did not want to deal with unpleasant circumstances.

Perhaps Mark quit because of *satisfaction*. After the successful work in Cyprus, Mark felt they had done enough. Many had been won to the Lord. Much good had been done. He felt like he had done enough for God.

Perhaps Mark quit because of *spite*. In the early going, Barnabas was in charge. Throughout Cyprus we read about the adventures of Barnabas and Paul. Then, we notice a subtle shift in authority. Luke began to write about Paul and Barnabas. Mark, who was kin to Barnabas, may have become disturbed by the usurping of power by Paul, and he went home in a fit of anger.

We cannot control what happens to us. However, we alone control how we respond to what happens to us. Conflict can destroy us or develop us. We can allow it to make us bitter or better.

The Communication (13:14-52)

When Paul and Barnabas arrived at Antioch of Pisidia, they once more preached the gospel. The communication was given in two different directions.

1. To the Jews (13:16-43)

The missionaries began their communication to the Jews. Luke said, "They went into the synagogue" (13:14). This was Paul's pattern, to begin with the Jews, normally, in the synagogue. Why? One motive was to show the local authorities the Christian faith was not a new religion but an outgrowth and culmination of Judaism. Paul was also motivated by a deep concern for the Jews.

The message was the same basic gospel Paul had preached in other places. We see the analysis of Jesus' life (13:23-31), the element of fulfillment of Old Testament prophecies (13:32-37), and the call to decision (13:38-41). We also see the same mixed reaction from the Jews: reception by some (13:43) and rejection by others (13:45). With the adverse reaction of the Jews, Paul turned to the Gentiles.

2. To the Gentiles (13:44-52)

Paul declared his justification for turning to the Gentiles. For one thing, the Jews had rejected his message (13:46). For another thing, the Scripture predicted God's message would be for all people (13:47). The response of the Gentiles to the gospel was overwhelming.

Jealous of the response of the Gentiles, the Jews stirred up the people against the missionaries. As a result, Paul and his entourage were forced to leave. As they left, they shook the dust off their feet, a gesture Christ commended to His disciples when they left an inhospitable place. Don't miss the note of satire. To shake off your dust meant you were breaking off all social contact. Among the Jews, that was tantamount to calling a person a heathen. The Jews ran Paul out of town for preaching to heathens. By shaking the dust off his feet, Paul informed the Jews that they were the real heathens.

The Confession (14:1-20)

The Bible contains many great confessions. In the Old Testament, there is the great confession of Israel called the Shema: "Hear, O Israel: the Lord our God is one Lord: And thou shalt love the Lord thy God with all thine heart, and with all thy soul, and with all thy might" (Deut. 6:4-5, KJV). In the New Testament, there is the confession made by Peter at Caesarea. When speaking for the disciples, he declared to Jesus, "Thou art the Christ, the Son of the living God" (Matt. 16:16). Equal in importance to these two majestic confessions is the confession that is found in our text—the Lycaonian confession. The Shema was a confession about God. The Caesarean confession was a confession about Jesus. The Lycaonian confession was a confession about humanity.

Let me set the scene. When the initial success at Antioch of Pisidia was replaced by hostility, Paul and Barnabas were forced to leave the city. They journeyed to Iconium where opposition again forced them to leave. Acts tells us they then fled to the cities of Lystra and Derbe, located in the region of Lycaonia (14:6).

In Lystra, Paul healed a man who had been lame all of his life. The result was exultant joy throughout the city. "The gods have become like men and have come down to us" the people said, referring to Paul and Barnabas (14:11). Even the local pagan priests were ready to offer sacrifices to Paul and Barnabas (14:13). This is the background for the Lycaonian confession in Acts 13:14-15. When the people were ready to worship them as gods, Paul and Barnabas declared, "We are also men of the same nature as you." This confession at Lycaonia was a confession of their humanity. This is a confession that needs to be made in the church today, because it speaks directly to the two vital dimensions of our lives.

1. Our Relationship to Others

In our relationship with other people, we often go to two extremes. Both extremes are seen in our text. When the citizens of Lystra thought more highly of Paul and Barnabas than they should, the people wanted to worship them (14:13). When they thought more lowly of Paul and Barnabas than they should, the people wanted to kill them (14:19). We see the same extremes in our relationship with people today. We judge people as being better or worse than us and determine our relationship to them accordingly.

An air force officer was promoted and assigned to an important office in the Pentagon. On his first day, he was very nervous because he wanted to impress everyone about his importance. However, he was not really sure what he was supposed to do. As soon as he sat down at his desk, the officer heard a knock at the door. The new official wanted to impress his first visitor, so as he said, "Come in," he reached over to pick up the phone, which had not rung, and put it to his ear. A young man entered the office. The new official said with a commanding note in his voice, "Just a minute, son. The phone rang just as you knocked." Then he began to speak into the phone, "Yes, sir, general. I'll do it right away. I'll call the president right now and take care of it. Thank you for your confidence in me, general. Goodbye." He hung up the phone, looked at the young man, and said, "Now, son, what is it you want?"

The young man answered, "Sir, I just came in to connect your telephone." Very often, we are so intimidated by others that we seek to impress them with our own importance, trying to lift ourselves to a higher level.

Even more damaging are our attempts to bring other people down to our level through criticism. One of the most destructive forces in the church today is the critical spirit. Our churches are filled with people in "God's Gestapo," committed to criticizing everyone and everything they can. They are critical about how we dress, how we talk, how we live, how we rear our children, and how we spend our time. They express their criticism by malicious gossip, snide remarks, and anonymous letters. The motivation for such a critical spirit is envy and jealousy, the deadly duo, which people use to bring others down to their level.

The Lycaonian confession reminds us that all of us are on the same level. There are not some above us who are more important to God or some below us who are less important to God. We are all men and women of the same nature.

2. Our Relationship to God

A lot has been written and said in recent days about the philosophy of life called "humanism." This philosophy, which declares "no deity will save us; therefore, we must save ourselves," is rooted in the belief that there is no God. Humanism and atheism are two sides of the same coin. Not many in America today would claim theoretically to be atheists or humanists. However, millions of Americans are practicing atheists and practicing humanists, because in their daily lives, they live as if God was not important and as if human beings were the hope of the world.

The Lycaonian confession calls us to accept our humanity and our dependence on God; it leads us to a new awareness of the sovereignty of God. Paul began by saying, "We are also men of the same nature as you." Then he added, "We . . . preach the gospel to you in order that you should turn from these vain things to a living God, who made the heaven and the earth and the sea, and all that is in them" (14:15). Paul took the focus off of himself so that he could put the focus on God. He was saying, "Human beings are not to be worshiped, but God is. Humanity is not sovereign, but God is."

In our day, we need to rediscover the fact that God is in charge of the world. He is the One who created the heavens and earth. He is the One who sets the agenda for history. He is the One who controls human destiny. He is the One who put the stars in space and holds the planets in place. He is the One who is to be worshiped. He is God—the God of the cosmos and of the atom, the God of the infinite and the infinitesimal, and the God of the telescope and of the microscope. He is God, not us. How we need to rediscover that truth today.

Conclusion (14:21-28)

Having completed the first missionary journey, Paul and Barnabas returned to the churches for a time of strengthening. This strengthening involved three things.

1. Warning

Paul was honest with the believers about what they would face as Christians. He said, "Through many tribulations we must enter the kingdom of God" (14:22). God does not promise to deliver us from difficulties, but He does promise to deliver us through our difficulties. In response to the health-and-wealth gospel, we need to proclaim the biblical message that suffering comes even to faithful followers of Jesus.

2. Organization

Paul was also honest with the believers about how they were to function. Paul firmly believed the Christian life had to be lived in fellowship with other Christians. Being a lone ranger Christian is not an option. One who is related to Christ must also be related to Christians. The fellowship of the church was important. Therefore, keeping the fellowship strong and vital demanded organization, so Paul "appointed elders for them in every church" (14:23).

3. Commitment

The most important ingredient in the church, however, was not organization but commitment. The Source of all power and wisdom is God. The only way these Christians could carry out their assignment was in a vital relationship with the living God. Therefore, Paul "commended them to the Lord in whom they had believed" (14:23).

10 | A Decision of Destiny

Acts 15:1-39

A professor in New York City decided to consult a psychiatrist. He chose one on Park Avenue. When the professor entered the office, he found himself in a beautiful reception area. However, no receptionist was there. He looked around and spotted two doors. Over one door was a sign that said "Men." Over the other door, the sign said "Women." He entered the door marked "Men" and found himself in another reception area, beautifully decorated with no receptionist. Again, the man saw two doors. One was marked "Introvert," and the other was labeled "Extrovert." After considering the options, the professor entered the door marked "Introvert." He found himself in yet another reception area, beautifully decorated, again with no receptionist. Sure enough, he spotted two more doors. Over one was this sign: "Those making more than $50,000 a year." Over the other door was this sign: "Those making less than $50,000 a year." The professor did not have to think about those options. He entered the door marked, "Those making less than $50,000 a year." He found himself back on Park Avenue! Choices! We all have to make them. Some are insignificant choices. Others are choices of monumental importance.

Churches also make choices. Churches usually make these choices at church conferences. Decisions are made at church conferences which decide the direction and destination of congregations. Perhaps, the most important church conference in all of Christian history was the great Jerusalem conference, because at this gathering of Christians, a decision of destiny was made. What happened? And how does it relate to us today?

The Setting (15:1-6)

Most scholars date this Jerusalem conference around A.D. 48. What was happening in the church at that time? The primary development was the spread of the Christian faith to the Gentiles. At first, all the believers were Jews. They were committed to the Jewish law and continued Jewish customs. They were Jews who became Christians. Then, the Christian faith began to expand beyond the boundaries of Jerusalem and beyond the ranks of the Jews. We read about Philip's experience with the man from Ethiopia (Acts 8), Peter's experience with Cornelius (Acts 10), then the emergence of a Christian church at Antioch (Acts 13), and the mission trip to Cyprus and Asia Minor (Acts 13). In each of these cases, not only Jews, but also Gentiles were brought into the church. This rapid progress of Gentile evangelization presented the more conservative Jewish Christians with a serious problem. Before long, more Christians would be Gentile than Jewish. The Jewish Christians were afraid the influx of so many Gentile believers would bring about a weakening of moral standards and a deterioration in the church. How could the new situation be controlled?

The members of the Jerusalem church had a simple solution. Gentiles should be admitted to the church on terms similar to those required of proselytes to Judaism. They must be circumcised and assume the obligation to keep the Mosaic law. If Paul and Barnabas neglected to bring the requirement of the law to the attention of the new Gentile converts, some in the Jerusalem church were prepared to correct the situation. Certain of these men came to Antioch to teach the Gentile brethren that unless they were circumcised and submitted to the law of Moses, they could not be saved.

This new teaching disturbed the Christians at Antioch and angered Paul and Barnabas. A heated discussion followed with Paul and Barnabas on one side and these new teachers from Jerusalem on the other side. The issue was not being settled, but rather antagonism was developing on both sides. Thus, the brethren in the church at

Antioch commissioned Paul and Barnabas to go with these teachers to Jerusalem and settle the issue. The result was the Jerusalem conference which is described in the fifteenth chapter of Acts.

Two questions were at stake. The primary question was the question of salvation: What was the requirement for salvation? A corollary question was the question of fellowship: What was required for all Christians to enjoy fellowship with each other?

The Support (15:7-18)

Paul believed faith alone was required for salvation. Gentiles could be saved by faith in the same way Jews were. Some in the church took another position. They required adoption of Jewish standards in addition to faith. In the Jerusalem Council, each side of those issues had support. Luke, however, concentrated on the support for Paul's side.

Simon Peter gave the personal testimony of his experience with Cornelius (15:7-11). Peter said Cornelius and his family, who were Gentiles, were saved without becoming Jews, a fact confirmed by the gift of the Holy Spirit to them. To say their salvation was not genuine, Peter concluded, was to question the character of God.

Paul and Barnabas had their turn. They told of their work among the Gentiles and explained how the validity of their work was confirmed each step along the way by God Himself (15:12).

James added his testimony. Drawing together quotes from Amos 9:12, Jeremiah 12:15, and Isaiah 45:21, he concluded that what was happening was nothing less than a fulfillment of what the prophets had foretold many centuries before (15:13-18).

Other opinions were given at this church conference. Luke clearly implied the weight of the testimony was in support of Paul's position.

The Solution (15:19-35)

After hearing all the evidence, James (who was evidently the moderator of the conference) led the church to a decision.

On the matter of salvation, the decision was unequivocal. No further burden would be placed on the Gentiles. No further requirement would be added. What must persons do to be saved? They must believe in the Lord Jesus Christ. That was all (15:19).

On the matter of fellowship between Jewish and Gentile Christians, the solution was not so simple. In order to facilitate fellowship between these two groups, four basic guidelines were suggested. Three of these had to do with table fellowship. The other related to moral character. These four suggestions had nothing to do with salvation. They related to fellowship between those who were already saved (15:20).

This decision of the Jerusalem Council, that was communicated to the Gentiles in the form of a letter, brought two results.

1. Gratitude (15:31-34)

Consternation was replaced by encouragement when the Gentile Christians heard the result. The genuineness of their salvation experience was recognized. In addition, they welcomed the suggestions to strengthen their relationship with Jewish Christians. Luke said, "When they had read it, they rejoiced because of its encouragement" (15:31). The attitude of gratitude is a healthy approach to life because gratitude toward God does three things for us.

First, gratitude toward God *humbles us.* Each of us has a tendency to think more highly of ourselves than we should. We're like the little boy who was riding in the back seat of the car. Suddenly, the door came open. He held on to the door until the mother could slow the car down. Thus, he escaped serious injury. That night, the mother said, "Son, you need to thank God for saving your life today."

The boy responded, "Why should I thank Him? I'm the one who held on." When we realize that all we have comes from God and respond to Him with gratitude, it will correct our opinion of ourselves.

Second, gratitude toward God *blesses Him.* When Jesus healed the ten lepers, only one returned to thank Him. Jesus said, "Were there not ten cleansed? But the nine—where are they? Were none found who turned back to give glory to God, except this foreigner?" (Luke 17:17-18). Our gratitude brings honor and glory to God.

Third, gratitude toward God *makes us more appreciative.* A gracious attitude is contagious. Gratitude toward God creates a sense of gratitude toward others. Perhaps, that is the secret of Mother Teresa. She spends an hour and a half each day in prayer to God. That time in the presence of God transforms her heart and energizes her spirit. The result is an unqualified compassion for hurting humanity.

2. Growth (15:35)

The decision of the Jerusalem Council opened the door for Gentiles to become Christians on the same basis and with the same status as Jews. Thus, Paul and Barnabas continued preaching the gospel to the Gentiles. Luke said, "But Paul and Barnabas stayed in Antioch, teaching and preaching, with many others also, the word of the Lord" (15:35). Luke did not specifically mention the results, but in the Book of Acts, whenever the gospel was preached, results came.

At the annual associational meeting, churches were giving reports. One pastor gave this report about his church: "Baptisms—none. Additions—none. Mission gifts—none. Dismissals—none." Then, he said, "Brethren, pray for us that we may hold our own!" God doesn't want us to hold our own. He wants us to grow. Growth comes when we share the gospel.

The Significance

The Jerusalem conference was an epoch-making event. The Jerusalem conference stands at the apex of the Book of Acts. Everything up to this point leads to this decision which, in turn, shapes the remainder of the story. The Jerusalem Council was one of the most significant church conferences in all of Christian history. Why was this conference so significant, and why is it significant for us today? This conference was significant because of what was decided about salvation.

1. The Recipients of Salvation

The good news of Jesus Christ is that God so loved the world. Jesus was lifted up so that all people might be drawn unto Him. The theme song of the church is "Whosoever will," may come.

A preacher explained to a group of children how the veil in the temple that separated the outer area from the holy of holies was split as Christ hung on the cross. "How big was the hole?" asked one little boy.

The preacher responded, "Big enough for anyone to get through."

At that historic conference in Jerusalem, the church recognized and proclaimed there is no limit on God's love. Whosoever will, may come. That was a significant decision.

2. The Requirement for Salvation

These early Christians not only affirmed anyone can be saved, but also They confirmed that Jesus alone can save That is the requirement of salvation. Not Jesus plus baptism; not Jesus plus circumcision; not Jesus plus church membership; not Jesus plus a holy life; not Jesus plus anything—Jesus alone. At that historic conference in Jerusalem, the church recognized and proclaimed the only requirement for salvation was to believe in Jesus.

3. The Results of Salvation

What happens to Christians when they are saved? Behind the four guidelines for fellowship which were suggested to the Gentiles (Acts 15:20) is a basic presupposition. When persons become Christians, they will become a part of the fellowship of Christ. When persons become children of God, they will become brothers and sisters to the rest of God's children. When persons love Christ, they will also love the church.

To all of those lone-ranger Christians through the ages who claim Christ but reject Christ's people—all of these modern-day loners who declare they can be Christians without going to church—the Jerusalem conference confirmed the truth that the Christian faith is to be lived out in the context of church where we worship and work, study and serve, and flourish and fellowship with our brothers and sisters in Christ. We cannot live our Christian lives alone. We cannot stand alone. When we become Christians, we become a part of God's family. Therefore, we need to identify with, associate with, cooperate with, and fellowship with God's people.

The Split (15:36-39)

In his book *The Reputation of the Church*, G. Avery Lee cited four diseases which often strike the church: *sleeping sickness*, the disease of a church that falls asleep in the midst of possibilities for ministry; *cirrhosis of the giver*, the money malady of a church that practices improper stewardship and thus limits its ministry; *hardening of the hearteries*, the disease of the heart in which a church loses its compassion and concern for those who are in need; and *spiritual myopia*, the lack of vision that keeps a church from seeing the long-term possibilities for ministry.[1]

The first-century church was susceptible to these ecclesiastical infections as has been the church in every age. The scenario of Acts 1—15, however, shows how the church escaped each of these diseases. Sleeping sickness was not a problem in the early church because the Bible says, "Every day, in the temple, and from house to house, they kept right on teaching and preaching Jesus as the Christ" (5:42). Cirrhosis of the giver did not affect the church because the Bible says, "They began selling their property and possessions, and were sharing them with all, as anyone might have need" (2:45). The early church was not infected with hardening of the hearteries because the Bible says, "There was not a needy person among them" (4:34). They ministered to the physical as well as the spiritual needs of everyone. Neither did the church suffer from spiritual myopia because neither pain nor persecution, nor privation nor prejudice could dull their vision of what God was doing and would do through them.

The church, seemingly strong and healthy, undaunted by external threats, stood at the threshold of God's bright tomorrow. But, then, another disease infected the church, the disease I call *conflictitus*.

The missionary spirit tugged at Paul's heart again, so he said to Barnabas, "Let us return and visit the brethren in every city in which we proclaimed the word of the Lord and see how they are" (15:36). Then came the rift. Barnabas said he wanted Mark to go with them. Paul said if Mark was going, I'm not going. So sharp was the dissension between them that the Bible says, "They separated from one another" (15:39). Barnabas took Mark and headed in one direction. Paul took Silas and headed in another direction. Two great Christians were in conflict.

1. The Reality of the Conflict

Down through the centuries, Christians of all varieties have known the reality of conflict. In the early days, major differences led to the establishment of the Eastern church centered in Constantinople and the Western church centered in Rome. The Protestant movement was given birth in the crucible of conflict. Rather than acquiescing to the status quo, Martin Luther posted his famous ninety-five theses on the door of the Castle Church in Wittenberg in 1517. In the midst of this conflict, Luther was excommunicated from the church, and Protestantism was born. The Anglican church was born in the midst of a political conflict between the ruler of England and the Pope in Rome. Then, the Methodist church grew out of the internal conflict of the Anglican church. On and on the story goes.

Conflict between Christians has been a reality throughout Christian history. This should not surprise us because at the beginning of the church's history, among two of the choicest of God's saints, conflict broke out. This was not a mild disagreement but a serious rift. The word *paroxusmos* means an angry dispute or a sharp contention (15:39). Paul and Barnabas, two brothers in the Lord who had prayed together, cried together, shared victories together, and overcome hardships together, experienced such a deep conflict that they separated from one another.

Conflict is an inevitable part of life. We must never allow the fear of conflict to prevent us from doing what God wants us to do. It was true of the early church. It will be true of the church in every age.

2. The Reasons for Conflict

In the experience of Paul and Barnabas, we see the three basic causes of all conflict in the church.

The first cause of conflict is *personality.* God made us all different.

That's what gives life its spice. That is also what causes the sparks. The clear indication of the text is that Paul and Barnabas split over a personality difference. At the heart of Barnabas's personality was a kindness and tenderness which desired to give Mark a second chance. Paul's personality was marked by intensity, even sternness, which made him refuse to deal with Mark anymore. Whenever these two different kinds of personalities meet on a single issue, conflict is the result.

A second cause of conflict is *policy.* Some scholars suggest that the conflict between Paul and Barnabas went deeper than a matter of personality. In Galatians 2:13, we see that Barnabas refused to eat with uncircumcised Christians. In certain areas of his life, Barnabas evidently had policies that determined his actions, policies that were different from Paul's. Paul's policy was unlimited fellowship among Christians. He felt compelled to act on the basis of that policy in his relationship with the Gentiles. Barnabas had some hesitancies at this point. Not just a matter of personality but also a matter of policy led Paul and Barnabas to split.

A third cause of conflict is *pride.* Barnabas had been Paul's spiritual mentor, practically his father in the faith. Now, Paul had risen to pre-eminence and that, perhaps, bothered Barnabas. Maybe Paul felt Barnabas and Mark, as family members, would team up to create problems for his leadership. Pride could have been a factor on both Paul and Barnabas's side.

These three elements—personality, "who's in charge"; policy, "how things are done"; and pride, "who gets the credit"—are at the heart of conflict in the church.

3. The Result of Conflict

This split between Paul and Barnabas seemed to be a tragic hour for the early church. Instead, in His infinite wisdom, God produced a miracle of grace out of this human conflict. What seemed like a negative experience for the church, instead, produced several positive benefits.

The conflict led to an *increase in missionary teams*. Instead of one missionary team, now there were two. Barnabas and Mark shared Christ in Cyprus, and Paul and Silas preached in Asia Minor. The mission outreach was doubled.

The conflict led to an *involvement of Silas.* Silas was not only a faithful companion to Paul but also later a co-worker with Peter and probably the secretary who put to paper the First Epistle of Peter that is included in our New Testament. Had Paul and Barnabas not split, perhaps Silas would never have had the opportunity to become so deeply involved in God's work.

This conflict led to an *influence on Mark.* Chrysostom, one of the most preeminent of the early church fathers, claimed the conflict between Paul and Barnabas was of great service for Mark. The sternness of Paul, said Chrysostom, brought about a change in Mark's mind, while the kindness of Barnabas kept him from feeling abandoned.[2] Had Paul and Barnabas not split, Mark might never have had a second chance to prove himself.

The decision of the Jerusalem Council opened the door to world evangelism. Now with two missionary teams, the work of evangelism could proceed more rapidly.

11 On the Road with Paul

Acts 15:40—18:22

At 3:00 one cold morning, a missionary candidate walked into an office for a scheduled interview with the examiner of a mission board. He sat in the waiting room until 8:00 a.m. when the examiner finally showed up. Without a word of explanation about his five-hour delay, the examiner said, "Let's begin the test. First, please spell *baker.*"

The young man responded, "B-a-k-e-r."

"Very good," responded the examiner. "I'm impressed. Now, let's see what you know about figures. How much is two plus two?"

The applicant replied, "Four."

"Fine," the examiner said. "You have passed the test. I'll recommend to the board tomorrow that you be appointed." At the board meeting the next day, the examiner spoke highly of the applicant. He said, "He has all the qualifications of a missionary as I discovered in my test. First, I tested him on self-denial. I told him to be at the office at 3:00 a.m. He left his warm bed and came out in the cold without a word of complaint. Then, I examined him on patience. I made him wait five hours to see me. I tested him on temper. He failed to show any sign of it. He did not complain and did not question my delay. Finally, I tried his humility. I asked him questions a small child could answer, and he showed no offense. He has all the characteristics to be the kind of missionary we need."

Paul was a man uniquely endowed with the characteristics needed to be a missionary. In this chapter, we will go on the road with Paul.

The Missionary Team (15:40—16:5)

Paul did not carry out his missionary conquests alone, but rather, he gathered around him a fabric of friends with whose cooperative support he carried out his work. We are introduced to some members of the team.

1. Silas (15:40-41)

Barnabas and Paul split because of their differences over John Mark. Paul needed a new partner. The Bible tells us he chose Silas (15:40). What do we know about Silas?

First, Silas was a man of *commitment*. The decision of the Jerusalem conference needed to be delivered to the Gentile Christians at Antioch. Such an important mission required important emissaries. Silas was one of the messengers. Luke included Silas in the "leading men among the brethren" (15:22).

Second, Silas was a man of *compassion*. He delivered the church's decision to the Christians in Antioch. However, he was not satisfied with simply delivering the message. He saw work to be done. He became aware of needs to be met. So he "encouraged and strengthened the brethren" (15:32) and "spent time there" (15:32) with the Christians at Antioch.

Third, Silas was a man of *courage*. When Silas agreed to be Paul's companion on the new mission venture, he was under no illusion regarding the challenge before him. His opportunity to serve with Paul came because of the split between Paul and Barnabas. If such a man as Barnabas had quarreled with Paul, how could Silas get along with him? That thought must have gone through Silas's mind. Yet, he consented to go because he was confident God would provide.

We do not have a record of all of Silas's accomplishments. We know he accompanied Paul on this second missionary journey. He suffered and toiled side by side with Paul. Paul associated Silas with himself and Timothy in the opening salutations of the two Epistles to the Thessalonians (Silvanus was the Roman form of his name). Peter described Silas as a "faithful brother" (1 Pet. 5:12). This man of commitment, compassion, and courage was a part of the team on this second missionary journey.

2. Timothy (16:1-3)

John Mark's assignment on the first missionary trip was to disciple the new converts. Because Paul did not allow John Mark to participate in this second missionary journey, he needed a new helper. He chose Timothy. What do we know about Timothy?

Timothy was *produced by a woman of God*. Paul later wrote of his companion, "For I am mindful of the sincere faith within you, which first dwelt in your grandmother Lois, and your mother Eunice" (2 Tim. 1:5). This is "spiritual genetics." Part of the explanation for Timothy's character is that he had a mother who loved the Lord and was willing to share that faith with her son. She provided Timothy the unparalleled privilege of a Christian home. The home should be a hothouse where in the isolation of sheltered loyalties and beautiful things are grown that afterwards can be transplanted and applied to the common good of humankind. What kind of values are you transmitting to your children?

Timothy was *perfected by the Word of God*. Paul said of Timothy, "From childhood you have known the sacred writings which are able to give you the wisdom that leads to salvation through faith which is in Christ Jesus" (2 Tim. 3:15). Timothy's faith was perfected by the constant nourishment of God's Word.

A little boy learned a memory verse every week in Sunday School. One day the child said to his father, "I never can remember my memory verses for long. What's the use of learning them?"

His father asked him to take the wicker wastebasket outside and fill it with water. He tried, but, of course, the water kept running through. Finally, the boy returned with the explanation, "This basket cannot hold water."

The father said, "You're right, son, the basket cannot hold water, and your mind cannot hold all of the verses you memorize. But I want you to notice how much cleaner the wastebasket is since you have allowed the water to run through it. That's what happens when the verses of the Bible go through your mind. They may not stay there long enough for you to remember them, but the more you allow them to pass through your memory, the brighter, the cleaner, and the fresher your mind will be."

Third, Timothy was *prepared for the work of God*. Luke said Timothy "was well spoken of by the brethren who were in Lystra and Iconium" (16:2). The Greek verb is in the imperfect passive tense. This means the good report was a continuous witness given of him. Already, Timothy had demonstrated his gifts in service for Christ. When Paul came to town, saw Timothy's work, and enlisted him to help, Timothy was ready for this big opportunity. Why? Because he had faithfully performed the little jobs.

The Divine Guidance (16:6-10)

As Paul did not carry out his missionary work alone, neither did he determine the direction of his missionary work alone. Instead, he moved in response to divine guidance. Luke said the Holy Spirit forbade Paul and his company "to speak the word in Asia" (16:6). Luke explained further that when Paul tried to go into Bithynia, "The Spirit of Jesus did not permit them" (16:7). Luke added that the missionaries went to Macedonia "concluding that God had called us to preach the gospel to them" (16:10). "Forbidden by the Holy Spirit," "The Spirit of Jesus did not permit them," "God had called"—all of these phrases suggest Paul moved forward under the direct guidance of God. How did God reveal His will?

Some suggest the Spirit directed Paul and his companions through the words of a prophet. Others feel the Spirit made His will known through their circumstances, either in the resistance from the Jews or a combination of political factors. Perhaps, Paul used his mind to discern the will of God. The word *concluded* (16:10) means "to agree or to arrive at a conclusion." It means to examine a matter and to put two and two together. Still others believe the Holy Spirit revealed His will to Paul through an illness. Luke also mentioned a vision given to Paul (16:9). Personalities, circumstances, intellect, suffering, and visions— all of these can be conduits through which God reveals His will to human beings.

The point is that Paul was spiritually sensitive enough to pick up on God's revelation. Because he was walking in the Spirit and because he was attuned to God, Paul was able to put two and two together and know what God wanted him to do.

Philippi (16:11-40)

God led Paul into Macedonia and to the city of Philippi. What a majestic city Philippi was. Nearby were the silver and gold mines which had made Philippi a great commercial center of the ancient world. Nearby in 42 B.C., Antony and Octavian had defeated Brutus and Cassius, a battle that determined the future shape of the Roman Empire. Philippi was located in the most strategic site in all of Europe, because a range of hills divided east from west and just at Philippi the chain of hills dipped into a pass so that the city commanded the road from east to west. Philippi was a Roman colony, a little bit of Rome planted in that part of the empire. As a bastion of Roman authority, the city of Philippi was one of the most important cities in the first-century world. Paul preached the gospel there and established a church in that city. Notice several characteristics of the church in Philippi.

1. Saved

Luke mentioned three particular individuals: the businesswoman Lydia (16:14), the possessed girl (16:16), and the crusty old jailer (16:27). These three were from different levels of society. They had different spiritual needs. They looked at life with a different perspective. The common thread which tied them together is that all three were saved by Jesus. This is not an exhaustive list of those who met the Lord at Philippi but merely a sampling. Luke included these three to explain that the church at Philippi was a church where people were being saved.

A group of tourists was enjoying a guided tour of one of the magnificent cathedrals in London. Pointing to one pew, the guide said, "That's the royal pew." Pointing to another, he said, "That is where the head of the British Parliament sits." Pointing to the pulpit, he said, "That is the most famous pulpit in the world." After extolling the virtues of the building, the guide asked, "Are there any questions?"

A young lady asked, "Has anybody been saved here lately?" That must forever be the question to the church: Has anybody been saved here lately? The Philippian church was a church where people were being saved.

2. Suffered

When Paul moved to the city of Philippi with the message of God's redeeming love on his lips, he was not rewarded with a ticker tape parade. He was not feted on the banquet circuit. He was not given the key to the city. Instead, he was harassed, falsely accused, beaten with rods, and thrown into jail. For Paul and his companions, being Christians involved suffering.

At a religious festival in a South American country, a series of booths lined the midway. One booth sold trinkets and necklaces. Printed on the front of the booth was a sign that said, "Cheap crosses here!" Many Christians today are looking for cheap crosses. They want discipleship without demand and sanctification without sacrifice. At Philippi, commitment to Christ resulted in suffering and sacrifice.

3. Sang

One of the most incredible verses in the Book of Acts is Acts 16:25. After having been beaten, after having been thrown into the dungeon, and after having been securely shackled, "about midnight Paul and Silas were praying and singing hymns of praise to God." Singing while they were suffering—what an incredible reaction to suffering!

E. Stanley Jones, famous Methodist missionary and world spokesman for Christ, related in his autobiography that he came early in his Christian life to a principle that was to be the central, driving force of his life. He decided he would not just bear occupation and difficulties. He would use them. He learned to sing in the face of suffering.[1]

In Philippi, suffering did not create despair but joy. These Christians in Philippi sang as they suffered.

4. Shared

After the jailer was saved, "they spoke the word of the Lord to him together with all who were in his house" (16:32). Paul and his company did not just endure their suffering. They did not just sing in their suffering. In the midst of their suffering, they continued to share the good news of God's love in Jesus Christ.

Several years ago, Paul Bell, a missionary in Bastrop, Texas, led a man to the Lord one day who was in his sixties. When the man was saved, he said, "I can't read or write, so I want you to teach me John 3:16 and a stanza of the song we sang today, 'What a Friend We Have in Jesus.' " He promised to come back to church to be baptized. Three weeks passed, and the new convert did not show up. On the fourth Sunday he came, along with five other men. All five walked the aisle. After the service, the convert turned to the missionary and said, "We are all here to be baptized." This new Christian lived only two years after that. By the time of his death, this old woodcutter had won fifty men to the Lord with one verse of Scripture and one stanza of a song.[2] Why? Because he was an eloquent speaker? Because he was a trained seminarian? Because he was an ordained clergyman? No, because he was willing to share his faith. In Philippi, Christians realized they were not just saved from something. They were also saved for something. Consequently, they shared their faith with others.

Thessalonica (17:1-9)

Originally named Therma for the hot springs adjacent to it, Thessalonica was the capital of the province of Macedonia. The population of 200,000 was a mixture of Greeks, Romans, and Jews. Thessalonica was the largest and most important of the cities located on the great Roman highway, the Egnatian Way. Thessalonica was Paul's next stop after leaving Philippi.

When the Christian missionaries came to Thessalonica, the Thessalonians declared, "These that have turned the world upside down

are come hither also" (Acts 17:6, KJV). Actually, these Christians
turned the world right side up. Where there was darkness, they
brought light. Where there was hatred, they brought love. Where
there was sadness, they brought laughter. Where there was chaos,
they brought leadership. Where there was bondage, they brought
liberation. Where there was death, they brought life. They took a
world that was troubled and tangled, and they turned it right side up.
They put it back on its feet. The Bible tells us the qualities which
enabled them to turn the city of Thessalonica right side up.

1. Integrity

The world in which Christianity was conceived was a world of in-
comparable immorality. Slavery was a universally accepted system.
Homosexuality was rampant. Sexual permissiveness was the rule of
the day. Human life was cheap. Pleasure was primary. Into that world
of immorality, Christianity introduced integrity. This commitment to
integrity was like a breath of fresh air to the Roman world.

A letter was written to Diognetus in the middle of the second century. The letter marveled that the Christians "have their meals in
common, but not their wives. They find themselves in the flesh, and
yet they live not after the flesh." With that kind of integrity Paul was
able to persuade many in Thessalonica to join the cause of Christ
(17:4). That's why they turned the world right side up. They pene-
trated their world with an integrity it had never witnessed before.

2. Intensity

These first Christian missionaries turned the world right side up
because they were men and women of one purpose. They were serious about the task God called them to do. They had intensity. Notice
the intensity of Paul. Luke said Paul "went to them, and for three
Sabbaths reasoned with them from the Scriptures, explaining and
giving evidence that Christ had to suffer and rise again from the
dead." Then Paul concluded, "This Jesus whom I am proclaiming to
you is the Christ" (17:2-3).

We have largely lost that intensity today. We have too many

church members at ease in Zion. We have too many deacons mired in the modicum of mediocrity. We have too many Sunday School teachers conspicuously captured by complacency. We have too many who have lost their intensity.

We need people with some intensity about the cause of Christ. The intensity growing out of the conviction that nothing is more important than the expansion of God's kingdom of earth was an essential ingredient enabling these Christians at Thessalonica to turn the world right side up.

3. Involvement

Several years ago, when the exploits of Albert Schweitzer in Africa were receiving international attention, a late night television personality made a statement that captures the spirit of our age. He told his television audience, "I'd like to be an Albert Schweitzer, if I could commute!" That is precisely what Christians cannot do. To carry out the work of Christ and to communicate the Word of Christ, we cannot commute. We must be involved in the church. To continue the witness of Christ and to conform to the will of Christ, we cannot commute. We must be involved in the world.

Paul was not a spectator at Thessalonica. He became involved. Luke said Paul went to the synagogue to speak to the Jews (Acts 17:2). He became involved with a great multitude of the God-fearing Greeks and a number of the leading women (17:4). Paul dared to get involved.

A group of middle-school youth prepared a Palm Sunday passion play to present to the church. They decided to read the Scripture passage, and then develop their own lines, expressing the Bible truths in their own words. When the boy playing Jesus came back to the disciples the second time, after praying apart from them in Gethsemane, he said, "Asleep again. Boy, they just don't make disciples like they used to!"

Do they still make disciples like they used to? Christian men and women who will demonstrate in their lives the integrity, intensity, and involvement of these early Christians? If so, then we will hear it

said of us what was said about the Christians who came to Thessalonica, "These people are turning the world right side up!"

Berea (17:10-15)

Berea was about fifty miles west of Thessalonica, south of the Egnatian Way. The city was relatively insignificant compared to Philippi and Thessalonica. Cicero called it "an out-of-the-way town."[3] Yet,
Luke described the Bereans as being "more noble-minded than those
in Thessalonica" (17:11). Since Paul sent no correspondence to the
Berean church, some conclude it must not have been very important.
Perhaps, Paul sent no correspondence to the Berean church because
these Christians preserved the faith and polity so well they did not
need a letter of correction or instruction. Notice the basic ingredients
of this Berean Church.

1. Progressiveness

The Bible tells us the Bereans were more "noble-minded than
those in Thessalonica" (17:11). Only two places in the New Testament is that word *noble-minded* used. The word means "well-born."
Eventually, the word was used to describe the disposition expected of
one so born. What disposition did Luke have in mind?

The Living Bible says the Bereans were "open minded." The Phillips
translation says they "proved more sympathetic." The *New English
Bible* says they were "more civil." The fullest meaning is seen in the
Amplified Bible that says, "They were entirely ready and accepted and
welcomed the message . . . with inclination of mind and eagerness."
These Christians at Berea were progressive. They were willing to hear
a new idea, flexible enough to consider a new plan, and compliant
enough to try a new way. They were progressive.

We live in a rapidly changing world. Ninety-five percent of the
science which will regulate life in America in the year 2000 is not
even known today. Every year we are confronted by tremendous
change. We can resist change as many churches have done in the past.
Or, we can, like the noble-minded Bereans, welcome change with
inclination of mind and eagerness of spirit because we recognize in

the new our only possibility of continuing to reach a changing world for Christ.

2. Priority

In facing change, we must avoid two extremes. We need to avoid the "Ponce-de-Leon anxiety." Ponce de Leon was a Spanish explorer who searched endlessly for the fountain of youth whose waters would return him to his youth, so he could enjoy the good old days of the past. The Ponce-de-Leon anxiety says "the old ways are always the best." Another extreme, equally dangerous, is "neolotry." Neolotry says "the new ways are always the best." Both extremes are to be avoided. How can we tell when the old ways are actually the best and when they are to be discarded? How can we discern when the new ways are the best or when they are to be resisted? Couched in the terms of Reinhold Niebuhr's famous prayer, knowing that some things need to be changed and that other things cannot be changed, how can we have the wisdom to discern between the two?

Notice what the Berean Christians did. Luke said, "They searched the Scriptures day by day to check up on Paul and Silas' statements to see if they were really so" (Acts 17:11, TLB). They had a priority by which their progressiveness was monitored: a commitment to the Word of God. The Scripture was the standard by which they determined the trustworthiness and viability of any new idea.

In response to the preaching of Paul at Berea, "Many of them therefore believed" (17:12). However, the Jewish religious leaders who opposed Paul—we call them Judaizers—followed him to Berea and again agitated the crowd. Paul left immediately for Athens and waited there for Silas and Timothy to join him.

Athens (17:16-34)

Few cities in the ancient world compared to the city of Athens. Educationally, it was the greatest university town in the world at that time. In the realm of religion, Athens was a great city of gods. Historians said a person could meet a god in Athens easier than one could meet a man. Philosophical debate dominated the time and energy of the leadership. The dialect used in Athens was the basis for the Koine Greek that became a world language under Alexander the Great. Few cities in the ancient world compared to the city of Athens. Waiting in Athens for Silas and Timothy, Paul's heart was agitated by the spiritual condition of the people. As he strolled up and down the streets of this commercial, intellectual, cultural, and financial center of the world, he was appalled at the rank immorality and rampant idolatry that dominated the life of the people. Luke said, "His spirit was being provoked within him" (17:16). What about the people provoked Paul? And what was his message to them?

1. The People (17:16-21)

Again, Paul started in the synagogue where he "was reasoning" with the Jews and the God-fearing Gentiles (17:17). He then carried his message out to the streets. How did the people respond?

They responded with *criticism*. Luke said they called Paul an "idle babbler" (17:18). The Greek word is *spermologos* which was used in reference to a sparrow who picked up scraps in the market place. They accused Paul of being an intellectual sparrow, picking up seeds of ideas here and there and then throwing them out to impress other people.

They responded with *confusion*. The Athenians thought Paul was preaching about "strange deities" (17:18). The word for resurrection is *anastasis.* Some scholars believe the Athenians considered *anastasis* to be the female counterpart of Jesus who was the male deity. No wonder they were confused.

They responded with *curiosity*. Paul was invited to speak to the Areopagus. This was the appointed spot for public gatherings to hear lecturers expound on many different ideas. The Athenians said to Paul, "May we know what this new teaching is which you are proclaiming?" (17:19).

2. The Proclamation (17:22-34)

Paul's message to the Athenians was a message about God. In the midst of their intellectual confusion and moral depravity, Paul felt the message they most needed to hear was a message about God.

Paul proclaimed a message about *an existing God*. These Athenians believed in the existence of gods. In fact, they had idols scattered all over the city. In case they forgot one of the gods, they added an altar to the unknown God. Paul began by saying that you are right on this point. The Athenians knew God existed. Paul simply needed to clarify their understanding about who God was. He said, "What therefore you worship in ignorance, this I proclaim to you" (17:23).

Paul proclaimed a message about *an eminent God*. Paul wanted them to know that this God who existed was one who stands above all other things in existence. He said God "made the world and all things in it" (17:24). He said that He is "Lord of heaven and earth" (17:24). He said that God had no needs but instead "He Himself gives to all life and breath and all things" (17:25). This God who exists is a great God. He is greater in wisdom than the combined knowledge of a billion Einsteins. He is greater in power than atomic and nuclear power combined. He is greater in authority than all the kings who have ever ruled. He is greater in love than the longings of a million mothers' hearts. He is an eminent God.

Paul proclaimed a message about *an embracing God*. Paul explained that this God was "not far from each one of us" (17:27). God's desire is that "in Him we live and move and exist" (17:28). This God who existed before all the universe and is eminent among all the powers of our world is a God who cares enough to come to us and embrace us so that in Him we can experience life.

Paul proclaimed the message about *an exacting God*. Paul concluded the message with a word of challenge. "Therefore having overlooked the times of ignorance, God is now declaring to men that all everywhere should repent, because He has fixed a day in which He will judge the world in righteousness through a Man whom He has appointed" (17:30-31). With the offer of new life from God comes the demand for a choice. Either we accept His gift in Christ, or we reject it. Christ then becomes the standard by which our lives will be measured.

Paul's message received the same mixed response in Athens that it received elsewhere. Some ridiculed Paul and rejected his message (17:32), while others believed Paul and received his message (17:34).

Corinth (18:1-17)

From Athens, Paul went to Corinth. Three words characterized the city of Corinth: *significant, syncretistic,* and *sensual.* Corinth was a significant city in the ancient world. Standing on the isthmus between the north and south parts of Greece, Corinth became the trade center of the Mediterranean. Corinth was also a syncretistic city. Corinth, perhaps more than any ancient city, displayed the kind of religious pluralism that is so prevalent today. Corinth was also a sensual city, known throughout the world for its wickedness. "To live like a Corinthian" was a proverb for loose living. The temple of Aphrodite fed this immorality. To the 600,000 people who lived in ancient Corinth, Paul brought the message of the gospel.

1. The Work Established (18:1-11)

Paul put down his roots in Corinth and for over a year and a half, he shared the message of Christ. Luke revealed some of the methods Paul used to establish the work.

The first key was *cooperation.* Luke introduced us to Aquila and Priscilla in verse 2. Who were they? Tradition suggests Priscilla was a Roman woman of a high-ranking position who married Aquila, a Jew. When the Jews were expelled from Rome, Aquila had to go. Priscilla, because of her love for Aquila, left her life of privilege and went with him. They became coworkers of Paul as he proclaimed the gospel to the city of Corinth. In addition, Silas and Timothy joined Paul to assist him in the work. They had remained in Berea when Paul went to Athens. Now, they rejoined him to continue the work. Paul recognized the city of Corinth could not be reached unless Christians worked in cooperation with other Christians who were committed to the same task.

The second key was *communication.* Luke said Paul "was reasoning in the synagogue" (18:4), "testifying to the Jews that Jesus was the Christ" (18:5), "speaking" (18:9), and "teaching the word of God"

(18:11). The focus of Paul's work was to communicate the truth of God. This communication was scriptural, "devoting himself completely to the word" (18:5); Christ centered, solemnly testifying "that Jesus was the Christ" (18:5); and was for all people, "trying to persuade Jews and Greeks" (18:4).

The third key was *continuation*. Paul was opposed by every power wickedness had at its disposal. He was ridiculed at every turn. He was attacked even by the power of the established religion. Yet, he did not quit. When the Jews ran him out of the synagogue, he set up a worship center in the house of Justus (18:7). When his opponents threatened him, he settled down for a year and a half (18:11). When he was dragged before Gallio, he remained many days longer (18:18). Paul did not give up.

With the assistance of Priscilla and Aquila, Silas and Timothy, and the new converts in the city, Paul continued to proclaim the gospel and established Christ's work in the city of Corinth.

2. The Work Opposed (18:12-18)

Paul's enemies appeared again. The charge against Paul was religious, but his enemies couched it in a political framework so that the Roman government would take action on it. They said, "This man persuades men to worship God contrary to the law" (18:13). Gallio refused to get involved saying, "I am unwilling to be a judge of these matters" (18:15).

Luke said, "They all took hold of Sosthenes, the leader of the synagogue, and began beating him in front of the judgment seat" (Acts 18:17). Who is "they"? Apparently these were Jews who were beating the leader of the synagogue. Why were they beating him? One leader of the synagogue had already been converted (18:8). Perhaps, Sosthenes also was leaning toward the Christian faith. The opponents of Paul used Sosthenes as an example of what they would do to any other Jews who embraced Christianity.

Paul was not frightened by their action. Instead, he "remained many days longer" (18:18), continuing to teach and preach the gospel of Christ to all who would listen, Jew and Gentile alike.

3. The Work Concluded (18:18-22)

While in Cenchrea, adjacent to Corinth, Paul "was keeping a vow" (18:18). During the time a vow was made, the hair would remain uncut. The cutting of the hair indicates that the period of Paul's vow had come to an end. What was his vow? We do not know. Luke is simply showing us that at the heart of Paul's faith was a constant, continuous, and oft-repeated commitment to God. George Gallup, Jr., has said about Christians today: "Many Americans belong to the 'not quite Christian' category; they believe, but without strong convictions. They want the fruit or reward of faith, but seem to dodge the responsibilities and obligations."[4] Paul did not belong to the "not quite Christian" category. His was a continuous and constant commitment to Christ.

Paul made his first contact with the city of Ephesus on his way back home after this second missionary journey. He initiated his work by going to the synagogue, yet he refused to establish a ministry in Ephesus. Instead, Paul left Priscilla and Aquila to begin the work. He would return soon.

When Paul reported on his glorious adventures for Christ, he went to both Jerusalem and Antioch. Antioch had become the center of this new spread of the gospel. Nevertheless, keeping contact with the Christians in Jerusalem was still important. At home in Antioch, Paul rested and revived his spirit. Soon, he would be back on the road again.

12 | Back on the Road Again

Acts 18:23—21:38

A reporter visited Mark Twain's haunts in Hannibal, Missouri, some years ago in order to gather material for a story on the famous writer, Samuel Clemens, who used the pen name Mark Twain. He found an old crony of Samuel Clemens who discounted the glory and fame of his former school friend. He said, "I knew as many stories as Sam Clemens. He just wrote them down!" There is a difference between knowing and doing. Many Christians know they need to go out into the world to share the gospel. Only a few actually do it.

Paul was one of those few. He constantly translated his theology into biography. He had a message, and he wanted to share it. Consequently, after spending some time in Antioch, he set off on another missionary venture. Luke told us Paul "passed successively through the Galatian region and Phrygia" (18:23). This phrase implies a definite order. Paul went systematically from church to church. What was his purpose? The Bible tells us he was "strengthening all the disciples" (18:23). Paul's purpose was to build up the brethren, to strengthen the churches, and to extend the work of Christ.

A Man with Potential (18:24-28)

Apollos is one of the most significant men in the New Testament. I've never met a person named for him. Yet, what he experienced needs to be experienced by every Christian in today's church. Apollos is a model for Christians in today's world because he matched his practice to his potential.

1. His Potential

What a remarkable person Apollos was! What potential he had! Apollos was *educated*. Luke said he was a Jew from Alexandria. Alexandria was the city of scholars who gave themselves to every sort of study. Luke added that Apollos "was mighty in the Scriptures" (18:24). He applied his mind to the study of God's Word.

Apollos was *eloquent* (18:24). This word describes his special gift for communication. He not only had knowledge. He was also able to express that knowledge in understandable and inspiring words. He was a communicator.

Apollos was *experienced*. Luke said he "had been instructed in the way of the Lord" (18:25). Perhaps, as a follower of John the Baptist, Apollos had become acquainted with the facts about Jesus and was proclaiming those historical facts to others. He was experienced in sharing his message.

Apollos was *enthusiastic*. Someone once asked Mark Twain the secret of his success. The famous humorist replied, "I was born excited." Apparently, so was Apollos. He was endowed with enthusiasm and excitement. Luke said he was "fervent in spirit" (l8:25). What potential Apollos had!

2. His Problem

Apollos' potential is obvious in the story. Two phrases in the text, however, cast a shadow over what otherwise is a bright portrait of a brilliant young Christian. Luke said Apollos was "acquainted only with the baptism of John" (18:25). Luke added, "When Priscilla and Aquila heard him, they took him aside and explained to him the way of God more accurately" (18:26). The point of these two phrases is that something was missing in Apollos' understanding. He knew the purpose of the Christian life. Apparently, he had not yet experienced the power with which to accomplish that purpose. He was aware of the judgment of God's holiness. Apparently, he had not yet experienced the joy of God's grace. He had a problem in his understanding, and he needed help. Apollos received help from Priscilla and Aquila.

Luke said, "They took him aside and explained to him the way of God more accurately" (18:26).

Picture the scene. On the one hand is Apollos, educated and erudite, holding people spellbound with his eloquence, riding a wave of popularity. On the other hand is an older couple, Priscilla and Aquila, taking him aside and saying, "Apollos, you are so gifted. God can really use you. But we've noticed some inadequacies, and we'd like to help you."

How would Apollos react? "Inadequacies in me? You've got to be kidding." Or, "Me learn from you? Who do you think you are to tell me what to say?" Or, "I have received my Ph.D. from the Alexandria Theological Training Center. What kind of degree do you have?" How easy for Apollos to have responded like that. The implication of the story is that Apollos listened, learned, and, then as a result, lived a better life. Because he understood that all of us can be taught and guided and helped by those who have been in the faith longer than we have, Apollos was able to match his practice with his potential.

A Group with Problems (19:1-7)

At a certain Christian school the teacher taught her class to repeat the Apostles' Creed, clause by clause, each pupil having his own clause. They would begin class each day with this group recitation of the Apostles' Creed. One morning, the recitation began with the first boy who said, "I believe in God, the Father almighty, maker of heaven and earth."

The second boy said, "I believe in Jesus Christ, His only Son, our Lord."

A sudden silence interrupted the roll call. As the teacher looked up to see what had happened, one of the pupils said, "Teacher, the boy who believes in the Holy Spirit isn't here today."

That is a precise description of these so-called disciples whom Paul encountered in ancient Ephesus. They claimed the name of Christ, but something was missing in their lives. That missing ingredient was the Holy Spirit. They said to Paul, "We have not even heard whether there is a Holy Spirit" (19:2).

Paul's response is often misunderstood. Paul did not say, "Have you received the Holy Spirit since you believed?" Instead, he said, "Did you receive the Holy Spirit when you believed?"

The Holy Spirit indwells the believer, every believer, at the point of conversion, not at some subsequent time. The very moment we claim Christ as our Savior and make Him our Lord, the Holy Spirit comes to dwell in our hearts. The difference is that in some Christians, the indwelling Holy Spirit has freedom to work. In others, the Holy Spirit encounters resistance. How do we resist the Spirit of God in our lives? Sometimes we grieve the Holy Spirit who is within us (Eph. 4:30). Sometimes we quench the Holy Spirit. (1 Thess. 5:19). Sometimes we can neglect the Holy Spirit (1 Tim. 4:14).

Many Christians in today's churches are living their Christian lives as if they did not even know the Holy Spirit existed. They are grieving the Spirit, quenching the Spirit, and neglecting the Spirit. There is a missing ingredient in their lives. The seriousness of the problem becomes apparent when we realize what happens when a Christian tries to live without the Holy Spirit.

1. Lack of Direction

When Jesus was preparing His disciples for His death, He gave them this promise: "I have many more things to say to you, but you cannot bear them now. But when He, the Spirit of truth, comes, He will guide you into all the truth" (John 16:12-13).

Jesus has given the Holy Spirit to every believer to guide each person into truth. The Holy Spirit guides us through God's Word, through our circumstances, through our sanctified common sense, through closed doors, and, sometimes, through our companions. When we grieve the Spirit, quench the Spirit, and neglect the Spirit, the result will be a Christian life with no clear direction and no precise purpose. Discipleship without the Spirit results in a lack of direction.

2. Lack of Dynamic

Just before Jesus left His disciples, He gave this promise: "You shall receive power when the Holy Spirit has come upon you" (1:8). Jesus has given us the Holy Spirit not only to direct our paths but also to provide the dynamic for victorious Christian living. The Holy Spirit not only wants to enlighten our minds but also wants to empower our hearts. When we grieve the Spirit and quench the Spirit and neglect the Spirit, the result will be a Christian life with no dynamic power and no victorious results. Discipleship without the Spirit results in a lack of dynamic.

Two things are needed in every Christian life: an accurate perception of life and an adequate power for life. Both are available through the Holy Spirit. When we misunderstand or misappropriate the Spirit, we, like those in Ephesus, will be a group with problems.

A Church with Purpose (19:8-40)

A certain mother was talking about her daughter to a friend one day. She said, "I want my daughter to have enough religion to make her respectable but not enough to make her uncomfortable." That is the kind of Christianity most people have—enough to make them respectable but not enough to make them uncomfortable. What happens when God's people really decide to get serious with God? Luke answered that question with the story of the church at Ephesus. This was a church with purpose. They were willing to get serious with God. Luke explained the results.

1. Proclamation (19:8-10)

Paul began his preaching in the synagogue, as was his custom. Then, he went to the school of Tyrannus and shared the gospel there. Luke said, "This took place for two years, so that all who lived in Asia heard the word of the Lord, both Jews and Greeks" (19:10).

Paul could not possibly have spoken personally to "all who lived in Asia" in two years. How did they hear? How was it that "all who lived in Asia heard the word of the Lord"? The Christians in Ephesus were so serious about their commitment to Christ that they talked about Him everywhere they went. Proclamation of the gospel was being made, not just by Paul but by all the Christians.

E. Stanley Jones was in India several years ago when the Hindu leaders were working on a new constitution for India. In the section relating to the rights of Christians and other religious groups, someone suggested Christians should have "the right to profess, practice, and propagate" their faith. Many of the Hindu leaders balked at the word *propagate*, because that meant the Christians were free to try to convert others. In the midst of the debate, one Hindu said, "The duty to propagate their faith is inherent in the Christian faith, so if you do not give the right to propagate, you do not give the right to profess and practice."[1]

When God's people get serious, they will inevitably share their faith with others, because the propagation of our faith is inherent in the practice of our faith.

2. Power (19:11-16)

The proclamation of the gospel resulted in remarkable achievements for Christ. Luke said, "God was performing extraordinary miracles by the hands of Paul" (19:11). When the Ephesians became serious enough about their faith to proclaim it to others, they experienced extraordinary miracles from God.

Many magicians and exorcists lived in the city of Ephesus, among them some itinerant Jews. One of these itinerant Jewish magicians was a man named Sceva. Luke described him as "a Jewish chief priest" (19:14). Sceva had seven sons who were also in the business of magic and exorcism. Seeing the great power Paul and the other Christians exhibited through the use of Jesus' name, they decided they would try it themselves. They approached a man with an evil spirit and pronounced piously: "I adjure you by Jesus whom Paul preaches" to come out (19:13). The masquerading magicians received a different response than they expected. The evil spirit responded, "I recognize Jesus, and I know about Paul, but who are you?" (19:15). Then the man with the evil spirit attacked the sons of Sceva and sent all seven scurrying for safety.

These sons of Sceva were not interested in Jesus. They were interested in themselves. They were not concerned about what they could do for Jesus. They were concerned about what Jesus could do for them. Jesus was nothing more than an Aladdin's lamp that could be used to promote their own welfare. They wanted to use Jesus. Like these seven sons of Sceva, people have tried to manipulate Jesus and counterfeit His power.

The message of our story is that Jesus cannot be manipulated. He is not an errand boy who comes at our beck and call. He is not an Aladdin's lamp we rub when we have a need. He is not our servant. He is our Lord! He is not to be used. He is to be worshiped, served, and obeyed. The power of Jesus cannot be counterfeited. This power comes to those, like the Ephesian Christians, who are willing to get serious with God.

3. Purification (19:17-20)

Exorcism was a popular occupation in ancient Ephesus. Evil spirits were blamed for all illnesses. Healing came from the exorcism of these spirits. Thus, a well-established exorcist trade existed in Ephesus. The experience of Sceva's sons revealed the foolishness of their incantations and magic potions. So, Luke said, "Many of those who practiced magic brought their books together and began burning them in the sight of all" (19:19).

Someone has suggested that eventually every person must either sacrifice his idols to his God or his God to his idols.[2] Many daily sacrifice their God to the idols of their lives. The Ephesians gladly, willingly, and daily sacrificed their idols to the God in whom their life was centered. When God's people get serious, like the Ephesians, they are willing to put out of their lives everything that stands as a barrier to their full commitment to Christ.

4. Problems (19:21-40)

Even Christians who are serious with God will be confronted by problems from those who are not serious with God. Thus, Luke said,

"About that time there arose no small disturbance concerning the Way" (19:23).

The leader of the opposition was a man named Demetrius whom Luke described as "a silversmith" (19:24). His speech indicated the irritation he felt over Paul's ministry. Demetrius and his friends were not opposed to Paul on theological grounds but on financial grounds. He said to his peers, "You know that our prosperity depends upon this business" (19:25). The spread of Christianity cut into the worship of Artemis. A decline in the worship of Artemis meant a decline in Demetrius's financial well-being. Therefore, he and his friends decided to take care of the problem.

Evidently, they could not find Paul. Instead, they grabbed two of Paul's companions, Gaius and Aristarchus, and dragged them to the theater. Paul's advisors would not let him go to the theater because the crowd was incensed. Ironically, most in the crowd did not even know what was happening (19:32).

One man, the town clerk, knew exactly what was going on. He saw the danger of a full-scale riot that would endanger his position and create long-term difficulties for the city. The clerk explained to the people the official avenue by which they could take care of such problems. After he clarified the issue, the crowd was dispersed.

When God's people get serious, vested interests are often threatened. Those who do not want to rock the boat are shaken. Those who are hanging on to the past are disturbed. Serious commitment to Christ does not remove problems. Sometimes, as it did for the Christians at Ephesus, it increases the problems.

A Missionary with Power (20:1-16)

Luke summarized in this section the continued missionary ventures of the apostle Paul. We see his spirit of encouragement (20:1-2). We see his cooperative work with other Christians (20:4). We see his commitment to sharing the message of Christ (20:7). We see the leadership of Paul as he made plans not only for himself but also for others in the missionary band (20:13). Mostly, we see his power. This power is demonstrated in an intriguing story that centers on a man named Eutychus.

1. A Remarkable Change

Luke said, "On the first day of the week, when we were gathered together to break bread, Paul began talking to them" (20:7). We do not know when the Christians permanently changed from worship on the seventh day of the week to worship on the first day of the week. We see evidence of the change quite early in the biblical account.

Why did these early Christians, mostly Jewish, change from the seventh day of the week to the first day of the week as their day of worship? Why did they turn from a tradition, deeply ingrained in their past, a tradition about which they were more adamant than about any other aspect of their religious faith? The answer is that the first day of the week was the day when Jesus arose from the dead, and they wanted to continually celebrate that event.

2. A Refreshing Custom

Luke said, "On the first day of the week, when we were gathered together to break bread, Paul began talking to them" (20:7). From the earliest days of Christian history the gathering of God's people for worship, fellowship, study, and encouragement has been the central most important habit in the Christian life.

To these first Christians worship was not an obligation but an opportunity. It was an opportunity to come into the presence of God and encounter Him in a fresh way. It was an opportunity to share a time of fellowship with the Christian family. It was an opportunity to bear one another's burdens through prayer and support. It was an opportunity to learn more about God's Word. What a blessed privilege!

Two words describe the choice open to every individual: *xenophobia* and *koinonia. Xenophobia* means the fear of that which is different from you and the tendency to pull away from it. That has been the way of the world from the beginning. *Koinonia* means fellowship with that which is different from you. According to the Bible, this is God's way.

3. A Regretful Calamity

What an opportunity Eutychus had! He was part of a group that gathered to hear from the great missionary Paul. He had the opportunity to hear firsthand of the initial developments in God's redemptive history in Christ. With that kind of opportunity, what did Eutychus do? He fell asleep (20:9).

A photograph in the newspaper showed a demonstration by the Royal Air Force of England. The photograph was of the VIP viewing stand. Queen Elizabeth was staring toward the sky. Prince Philip had his attention focused upward. In the middle was Frederick Mulkey, Britain's secretary of state for defense, with his chin resting on his chest, sound asleep!

What a picture of many Christians today. All around us, God is at work. Exciting things are happening. Opportunities for service abound. Demonstrations of God's power are everywhere. Yet, many Christians sit in the midst of these happenings sound asleep.

When Eutychus fell asleep, he not only missed the opportunity to hear the apostle Paul. He also fell out the window. The Bible tells us that Paul went down to Eutychus. He laid his own body on top of the lifeless body of Eutychus. He picked Eutychus up and embraced him. Then he announced that Eutychus would survive, and Eutychus did. Paul's life was so closely linked with the purpose of God that he became a channel for the power of God to work in the lives of others.

A Farewell with Passion (20:17-38)

On the way to Jerusalem, Paul stopped in Miletus. From there he sent word to the Ephesians. They came to Miletus for a passionate farewell before Paul left for Jerusalem. What would he say to his fellow Christians? Paul's sermon at Pisidian Antioch (13:16-41) is an example of his approach to the synagogue audiences. His sermon at Athens (17:22-34) is an example of his approach to pagan audiences. This sermon (20:18-35) is an example of Paul's message to Christian audiences.

1. His Past (20:18-21)

In the crowd of Christians from Ephesus were individuals who had been touched by Paul's past ministry. Lloyd John Ogilvie described the crowd as follows:

> Among them must have been some of the now Spirit-filled disciples of John on whom he had laid his hands at the beginning of his ministry in Ephesus; some transformed exorcists now liberated; a magician or two who had found a power greater than magic; a silversmith who no longer made silver images of Artemis to sustain his worship of the god of wealth; several leaders of the city who had found a Leader for their souls; criminals who had come to the city for asylum and discovered an eternal haven in Christ; and many cultists who had learned that Christ alone could satisfy.[3]

Paul summarized his past experience with the Ephesians. He outlined his allegiance to them (20:18), his humility among them (20:19), his courage before them, (20:20), and his love for them (20:21).

2. His Prospects (20:22-27)

As he looked to the future, Paul saw a dark cloud falling across his life. The Spirit of God had not promised Paul health and wealth. Rather, the Spirit had promised "bonds and afflictions" (v. 23). However, such prospects did not immobilize Paul, because his purpose was not to preserve his life but to fulfill God's purpose. Even though dangers were ahead, and even though he would never be able to see the Ephesians again, Paul moved forward because he wanted to complete the task to which he had been called: "to testify solemnly of the gospel of the grace of God" (v. 24).

Paul did not know what lay ahead. However, he knew that whatever it was, he had to face it, and he could face it because of his relationship with a God who was all-sufficient for every need.

3. His Practice (20:28-35)

Paul closed his message to the Ephesians by reminding them of his practice among them—to give of himself to them instead of taking from them. He said, "You yourselves know that these hands ministered to my own needs and to the men who were with me" (v. 34).

He included in these closing words a warning to the Ephesian Christians. "Therefore be on the alert," Paul told them (20:31). Dangers would be constant and continuous. They needed to watch lest they be led into temptation. He also said, "Be on guard for yourselves and for all the flock" (v. 28). As Christians, we are not only responsible for ourself. We are also to "bear one another's burdens, and thus fulfill the law of Christ" (Gal. 6:2).

Paul also included in these final words a reminder of the source of their power. He said, "And now I commend you to God and to the word of His grace, which is able to build you up and to give you the inheritance among all those who are sanctified" (v. 32).

In addition, we see the love of the Ephesians for Paul. They "began to weep aloud," they "embraced Paul," and they "repeatedly kissed him" (20:37). Because of all that Paul had done for them, the Ephesians were grieved that they would never see him again.

Paul left the Ephesians and headed for Jerusalem. What was Paul's purpose in going to Jerusalem? He wanted to try to reunite the church and to bring to realization God's desire to have both Jews and Gentiles together.

13 | In Defense of the Faith

Acts 21:1—26:31

Edward Everett, an outstanding orator and statesman of the nineteenth century, was approached by a man who complained that he had been libeled in a newspaper. He asked the great American for advice. Everett replied, "Do nothing!" And then he explained, "Half the people who bought the paper never saw the article. Half of those who saw it did not read it. Half those who read it did not understand it. Half those who understood it did not believe it. Half those who believed it are of no account anyway."[1] That's good advice, most of the time. However, on some occasions, criticism cannot be ignored. It has to be faced.

This was true for the apostle Paul. He had committed himself to the spread of the gospel, trying to ignore the critics. But the critics could not be silenced. They hounded him from one place to another. Finally, with his back to the wall, Paul stood his ground in defense of the faith.

Paul was warned several times of what awaited him in Jerusalem. As Paul visited the brethren in Tyre, they warned him not to go to Jerusalem (21:4). As Paul fellowshiped with the brethren at Caesarea, a prophet named Agabus provided a visual of the danger ahead for Paul in Jerusalem. Again, his Christian friends begged Paul not to go to Jerusalem (21:12). Paul's response is one of the most outstanding demonstrations of courage and commitment in the New Testament. Paul said, "I am ready not only to be bound, but even to die at Jerusalem for the name of the Lord Jesus" (21:13).

During the Civil War one dedicated Southerner said, "I would

151

rather die on my feet than live on my seat." This was Paul's conviction. He had an indomitable courage and sheer determination to go on. He was willing to defend the faith regardless of the cost. Paul's defense of the faith was given in several different settings.

Before the Brethren (21:1-40)

Paul returned from his third missionary journey with mixed reviews. Many were thrilled with his effectiveness for Christ. Others were concerned that he had gone too far in extending the gospel to all people. Before Paul defended the faith to the enemies of the church, he had to defend the faith before the brethren.

1. The Problem (21:1-14)

Paul's problem grew partially out of his *circumstances.* An explosive atmosphere prevailed at Jerusalem. The Jewish zealots were becoming more restless. Anything challenging the exclusiveness of the Jewish way and anything threatening the Jewish traditions was vehemently opposed. Paul's leadership in the ever-expanding Gentile mission put him in direct conflict with the prevailing mood among Jerusalem Christians. He stood for the right cause at the wrong time.

God has set into motion certain laws. Society around us generates certain moods. Heredity has endowed us with certain traits. As these natural laws above us, moods around us, and traits within us converge on our lives, we are often, like the apostle Paul, confronted by circumstances out of which trouble comes.

Paul's trouble grew partially out of his *companions.* Paul's critics followed him from place to place making life miserable for him. Trouble loomed large on the horizon for Paul because he was surrounded by people who were determined to give him trouble.

In Roman times certain magistrates, referred to as *censere*, were appointed to count the people and to supervise public morals. The *censeres* are still with us. Life is filled with censorious people who feel they are a cut above others morally and who believe they have been called by God to supervise public morals. Like Paul, our trouble often comes from such critical people around us.

Paul's trouble grew partially out of his *choices*. Paul could have avoided the trouble if he wanted to. If he had refused to preach to the Gentiles, he could have avoided trouble. If he had refused to go to Jerusalem, he could have avoided trouble. Instead, Paul deliberately chose to preach to the Gentiles and to go to Jerusalem. He chose a pathway that led to trouble.

Robert Louis Stevenson once wrote, "Everybody soon or late sits down to a banquet of consequences." Our choices, good and bad, put us on pathways where certain results inevitably come.

2. The Plan (21:15-40)

To add to his problems, Paul's critics spread a rumor that he had forsaken the commandments of God and had neglected the requirements of the law. A plan was suggested to solve the problem. Four men had apparently contracted some ceremonial defilement and had to undergo a purification rite in the temple. Seven days had to elapse, and then an offering was to be given. Paul's friends suggested he go to the temple and pay the expenses of their offering. This would confirm Paul's continued allegiance to the Jewish laws. Thus, the critics would be silenced.

Instead of commending Paul for following the Jewish custom, his critics found a supposed reason to condemn him. They mistakenly assumed Paul had taken a Gentile into the temple. They said about Paul, "He has even brought Greeks into the temple and has defiled this holy place" (21:28). His plan backfired. Things did not turn out like Paul planned.

Paul's critics stirred up such a frenzy among the people that they rushed Paul outside the temple to stone him. Notice the similarities between Paul's experience and the experience of Stephen. The same charge was made (6:13; 21:29). Paul began his defense with the same words Stephen used (7:2; 22:1). The difference was the Roman soldiers who came to Paul's defense. Paul's life was spared because God still had something for Him to do. The stage was set for Paul's defense against the enemies and critics of the gospel.

Before the Crowd (22:1-30)

An amazing transformation came over the crowd. At one moment they were ready to lynch Paul. At the next moment with a mere gesture of his hand, the crowd was silent and attentive to Paul's words. What a powerful personality Paul had. He was also a master communicator. We see this in his defense before the crowd.

1. Identification (22:1-5)

Paul realized that in order to communicate a truth to the crowd, he had to have their attention. He had to build some bridges over which his message could be communicated. He made contact at Athens by identifying with the Athenians' belief in God. He made contact here by identifying with the people. He identified with the people *linguistically*. Luke said that Paul began speaking to them "in the Hebrew dialect" (22:2). This was probably the Aramaic spoken by the common people of that day. He identified with the people *personally*. He called them "brethren" (22:1). He was not an enemy opposed to them but a brother related to them. Paul identified with the people *nationally*. He revealed that he too was "a Jew, born in Tarsus" (22:3). Paul was not an outsider. He was one of them. He identified with the people *educationally*. He was taught by one of the most respected of their teachers—Gamaliel (22:3).

By identifying with the people, Paul gained their attention. He was then ready to communicate his message.

2. Individuality (22:6-21)

After pointing out the similarities between himself and the Jews who listened, Paul then pointed out the differences. First, he explained that he knew God in a personal way and not just impersonally through the law (vv. 6-10). Second, Paul explained that he knew God in a life-changing way, as one who had been changed from the inside out (vv. 11-16). Third, he knew God in a universal way, as the Lover of the souls of all people and not just the Jews (vv. 17-21).

At that point, the crowd reacted with fury. Saying the word *Gentile*s was like lighting a fuse. The crowd exploded. Luke described the extent of their reaction, saying "they were crying out and throwing off their cloaks and tossing dust into the air" (22:23). Why did the crowd react with such violence? The key was Paul's decision to offer to the Gentiles what they thought was the exclusive right of the Jews: access to God. The Roman commander saved Paul from the crowd but was convinced Paul was guilty of some crime. As the commander prepared to examine Paul by scourging, Paul revealed that he was a Roman citizen. This frightened the commander because he could have been executed himself for beating a Roman citizen. Desiring to get to the bottom of the problem, the commander brought Paul before the Sanhedrin.

Before the Jewish Leaders (23:1-35)

The Sanhedrin still exerted strong influence over religious life in Jerusalem, so the Roman commander brought Paul before them to determine his crime. In his defense before the Jewish leaders, Paul revealed some things about himself.

1. His Emotion (23:1-5)

We often speak of the first-century Christians as if they were perfect saints, always under control with no emotion that was not held in check. The truth is these first Christians were just like Christians today. Paul was no exception. He was human, and in his humanity he could respond with great emotion. Paul began his defense by stating his commitment to God. The high priest gave an order to strike him. Paul responded, "God is going to strike you, you whitewashed wall!" (v. 3). When reminded that he should not speak to the high priest in such a tone, Paul responded, "I was not aware, brethren, that he was high priest" (v. 5). This could have been an expression of sarcasm in which Paul was saying, "I could not tell from his actions that he really was a high priest." Or it could have been an expression of ignorance in which Paul really said, "I did not realize the high priest was the one who gave the order."

The biblical writers did not whitewash the sins of the saints. The biblical writers discussed openly the drunkenness of Noah, the pride of Moses, the lust of David, the weakness of Samson, the fear of Elijah, the self-centeredness of James and John, and the inconsistency of Peter. Luke also revealed the emotions of Paul.

2. His Expedience (23:6-10)

Paul was always aware of the situations around him, and he used the circumstances to his advantage when he could. He saw both Pharisees and Sadducees in the meeting. Realizing their division over certain theological matters, Paul decided to redirect their attention from him to each other. So Paul declared, "I am a Pharisee, a son of Pharisees; I am on trial for the hope and resurrection of the dead!" (v. 6). The ploy worked, because a dissension arose between the Pharisees and Sadducees. Luke concluded, "The assembly was divided" (v. 7).

In one of His parables, Jesus told the story of an unrighteous servant who was fired by his master. However, before he lost his position, he made some deals to help himself out. Instead of condemning the unrighteous servant, Jesus commended him "because he had acted shrewdly." Then Jesus concluded, "For the sons of this age are more shrewd in relation to their own kind than the sons of light" (Luke 16:8).

That could never be said about the apostle Paul. With shrewdness Paul turned every situation to his advantage and to the advantage of the cause of Christ.

3. His Encouragement (23:11)

Near the end of his life, as a prisoner in Rome, Paul wrote a letter to the Philippians punctuated with joy. He explained the reason for his joy in the closing verses when he said, "My God shall supply all your needs according to His riches in glory in Christ Jesus" (Phil. 4:19). That was not a truth Paul read in a book. He discovered that truth in the crucible of life when difficulties, danger, and disappointment bombarded him from every direction.

This was one of the classroom sessions where Paul learned that truth. He was in a situation which looked hopeless from a human standpoint. In that situation, Paul received this word of encouragement from the Lord: "Take courage; for as you have solemnly witnessed to My cause at Jerusalem, so you must witness at Rome also" (v. 11).

4. His Enemies (23:12-35)

Paul needed that word of encouragement, because immediately he was confronted by his enemies who were determined to kill him. Luke did not identify these forty Jews who had made a vow to kill Paul. Nor do we know why they hated Paul so intensely. Paul had a personality that evoked an intense response of some kind, either intense loyalty or intense opposition. The interesting element in Luke's account is the introduction of a member of Paul's family. Since no other mention is made of Paul's family, scholars speculate that they disowned him when he became a Christian (Phil. 3:8). However, at least two members of the family still associated with Paul, his sister and her son. The young man heard about the plot to kill Paul and reported it to the commander.

The commander decided to send Paul to Caesarea and let Felix decide his case. Caesarea was the seat of the Roman government in Judea. Felix was the governor of the Roman province of Syria that included Judea. In his letter, the commander indicated the nature of the charges against Paul. They were religious charges from the Jews and not political charges from the Romans. The stage was set for Paul's next defense.

Before Felix (24:1-27)

Through family connections and political manipulations, Felix was appointed as governor of a Roman province. He was politically ambitious and morally unscrupulous. Representatives from the Sanhedrin, led by their spokesman Tertullus, traveled to Caesarea to present their charges.

1. The Accusations (24:1-9)

Tertullus announced the three charges against the apostle Paul. He accused Paul of *sedition*. He said, "We have found this man a real pest and a fellow who stirs up dissension among all the Jews throughout the world" (v. 5). He accused Paul of *sectarianism*. He called Paul "a ringleader of the sect of the Nazarenes" (v. 5). He accused Paul of *sacrilege*. He said, "And he even tried to desecrate the temple" (v. 6).

These accusations against Paul were marked by two things: flattery and falsehood. Tertullus, as a trained orator, knew the importance of complementing a man of such position and power as Felix. Both Tertullus and Felix knew the things he said were not true. It naturally followed that if the introduction was full of falsehood, the accusations were also full of falsehood. To see the falsehood of Tertullus's charges compare Luke's account of Paul's arrest (21:27-40) with Tertullus's account (24:6-8).

2. The Answer (24:10-21)

Paul denied the first and third charges. He pointed out he had only been in the city for twelve days, hardly enough time to stir up a riot (vv. 11-12). He challenged his accusers to bring proof of his sacrilege against the temple (v. 13). He went to the temple to worship God, not to profane God's house. He admitted to the charge of being identified with Jesus of Nazareth. However, Paul explained that legally being a member of this sect was no different than being a member of the Pharisees. He affirmed that Christians believed the same God as the Pharisees (v. 14), they believed the same Scripture as the Pharisees (v. 14), they held to the same doctrine of the resurrection as the Pharisees (v. 15), and they believed in the same purpose as the Pharisees— to have a clear conscience before God and men (v. 16).

The answers given by Paul were characterized by two things: tactfulness and truth. Paul did not sugarcoat his words with false flattery, nor did he bend the truth. Paul gave straight answers to his accusers.

3. The Abdication (24:22-27)

Luke said Felix had "a more exact knowledge about the Way" (v. 22). He understood the issue between the opponents of Jesus and the followers of Jesus was a religious question and not a political one. Felix could have settled the issue. He did apparently provide good conditions for Paul in his imprisonment. But he abdicated in his responsibility to free Paul. Why?

Felix did not free Paul because of his *fear*. The Bible tells us that as he talked with Paul "Felix became frightened" (v. 25). Partly, he was frightened at the thought of facing God. But some of his fear was politically motivated. He was responsible for keeping order among his Jewish constituency. If they created public unrest or if they reported him to Rome, Felix could be replaced as governor. Apparently, that happened two years later.

Felix did not free Paul because of his *procrastination*. Paul shared the message of Christ with Felix and his wife, and Paul pushed for a decision. Felix said, "Go away for the present, and when I find time, I will summon you" (v. 25). "When I find time" is the theme song of procrastinators. "Why do today what you can do tomorrow" is their philosophy. Some things can be put off without serious consequences. However, when Felix put off his decision about Christ, he missed his chance for eternity.

Felix did not free Paul because of his *greed*. Luke gave some insight into the character of Felix when he said, "He was hoping that money would be given him by Paul" (v. 26). His interest in Paul was mercenary. "What's in it for me?" was Felix's approach to life.

Notice the paradoxes of Felix's response. He was interested in treasure, but he let go of the treasure of the gospel. His name meant "happy," but he rejected the one pathway that would lead to true happiness. He sat in judgment of Paul, but in reality Paul was sitting in judgment of him. Felix presented the sad picture of a man who knew what was right but refused to do it, who trembled at the truth but refused to affirm the truth.

After two years, Felix's mismanagement and mistreatment of peo-

ple caught up with him. He was recalled to Rome, and only the plead-
ings of his brother kept him from being executed. When Festus suc-
ceeded Felix, Paul was still in prison. Festus was the next one before
whom Paul gave his defense.

Before Festus (25:1-22)

Festus immediately traveled to Jerusalem to become acquainted
with the leaders of the Jews, because they were his constituency. After two years, their bitterness toward Paul had not lost its intensity.
They reminded Festus of the need to deal with Paul. They requested
that the decision be made on their turf in Jerusalem. Instead, Festus
set up a meeting in Caesarea on his turf.

1. The Charges (25:7-8)

The charges were probably much the same as when the Jewish
leaders accused Paul before Felix two years earlier. Luke did not elaborate on the charges. In his response (v. 8), Paul implied that they
again charged him with sectarianism ("against the Law of the Jews"),
sacrilege ("against the temple"), and sedition ("against Caesar").
These charges were completely void of any proof, and Paul denied
them categorically.

2. The Compromise (25:9-12)

Because Festus recognized this was a religious issue, he suggested
that it be settled in Jerusalem before the Sanhedrin. However, because he recognized how volatile the issue was and how fraught with
danger for his position, he offered to be the judge.

Paul realized his dilemma. To go to Jerusalem was to go to his
death. Paul was not afraid of death, but his primary commitment was
to carry out the assignment God had given him. Therefore, Paul
called on a special privilege given to Roman citizens. If Roman citizens did not receive fair treatment in any of the provinces of the Roman Empire, they could appeal to Rome. This appeal took priority
over any other decision. Consequently, Paul's case would be heard
and handled by Caesar.

Why did Paul appeal to Caesar? One reason was his understanding of the Jews. He knew their intentions. Either death by an ambush along the way, or death by their judgment awaited him. Another reason was Paul's understanding of Festus. Felix had been an experienced administrator in Judea. Festus was a novice. Paul was afraid Festus would be manipulated by the Jewish leaders. A third reason was Paul's understanding of God's will. The Lord had promised Paul in a dream "as you have solemnly witnessed to My cause at Jerusalem, so you must witness at Rome also" (23:11). The fastest way to get there was to appeal to Rome.

3. The Consultation (25:13-22)

Festus had solved one problem only to be confronted by another. He would not have to decide whether to free Paul or turn him over to the Jews. Caesar would have to make that decision. However, when he sent Paul to Rome, he needed to include a specific charge which had been leveled against Paul. Festus was not sure what to write. He was saved from his dilemma by King Agrippa.

Galilee and Perea were combined in a kingdom which was ruled by King Agrippa II. This was the son of Herod Agrippa I, king of Judea from A.D. 41-44. He was more familiar with Jewish religion and more aware of the movement centered around Jesus. Agrippa offered to meet with Paul and advise Festus on the matter.

Before Agrippa (25:23—26:32)

Festus was counting on Agrippa to help him out of his dilemma. Festus clearly expressed the dilemma when he said, "For it seems absurd to me in sending a prisoner, not to indicate also the charges against him" (25:27). Again, Paul was called on to defend the gospel.

1. The Opportunity for Paul (26:1-23)

What would seem to some an obstacle was to Paul an opportunity. What would have created fear and uncertainty in some created a sense of excitement and anticipation in Paul. He had an opportunity to share the gospel with the king who would be most directly related to the Jewish leaders. This was an opportunity to win an influential man to Christ. Because of Agrippa's background, Paul hoped Agrippa would be persuaded by his explanation that Jesus fulfilled the hopes and dreams of the Jewish people. Even if he could not win Agrippa to Christ, at least he could explain to him what the Christian movement was all about. This might curtail future persecution against Christians.

Paul never balked when given an opportunity to preach about Jesus. In this defense before Agrippa, Paul developed the same themes with a slightly different outline.

He discussed his *context* (26:4-11). He described his Jewish upbringing and his status as a Pharisee. As a Jew he opposed the Christian movement and led in the persecution against them. Paul not only persecuted the Christians in Jerusalem and Judea. He also pursued them into the synagogues of Gentile cities. His life was set in the context of the Jewish faith.

He discussed his *conversion* (26:12-15). Paul's constant focus was on the Damascus road experience because that event changed his life and moved him in a new direction. What happened on the Damascus road? Paul met the resurrected Christ. He was given a new perspective, a new purpose, and a new power.

He discussed his *commission* (26:16-18). When Christ saved Paul, He gave him a task. Paul was to take the message of God's redeeming love to the Gentiles. As F. F. Bruce said, "That believing Gentiles were to have an equal and rightful share in the heritage of the holy people of God was a feature of the gospel which it was Paul's peculiar mission first to understand and make known."[2]

He discussed his *commitment* (26:19-23). Paul recognized that the primary ingredient in a committed life is obedience. Some do what is convenient. Others do what is expedient. Still others do what is profitable. Paul was committed to obeying God's will, even when it was not convenient, even when it was not expedient, and even when it was not profitable. Paul's life was characterized by a prayer I heard one time: "Dear God, may your will be done in my life, nothing more, nothing less, nothing else. Amen." To what was Paul committed? He was committed to proclaiming this truth about Jesus: "The Christ was to suffer, and that by reason of His resurrection from the dead He should be the first to proclaim light both to the Jewish people and to the Gentiles" (26:23).

2. The Objection of Agrippa (26:24-32)

Festus reacted with disbelief to the testimony of Paul and accused him of losing his mind. Paul was not concerned about Festus at this time but Agrippa. Paul confronted Agrippa with this challenge: "King Agrippa, do you believe the Prophets?" (v. 27).

He responded with a somewhat ambivalent answer: "In a short time you will persuade me to become a Christian" (v. 28). What did Agrippa mean? Was Agrippa sarcastic or sincere? Did he mean "you have just about persuaded me to be a Christian," or did he mean "do you think you can persuade me to be a Christian?" Was he saying "you have just about convinced me with your religious discussion," or "you don't think you are going to get me involved in that kind of religious discussion, do you?"

We don't know exactly what Agrippa meant. Two things, however, are clear from the passage. The first obvious fact is that Paul was in charge. Even as a prisoner before a governor of a province and a king of a nation, Paul as a prisoner was the dominant personality. The other obvious fact is the distinction between Paul's certainty and Agrippa's uncertainty. Paul knew who and what he believed. Agrippa was not willing to make a commitment. That is why, two thousand years later, we speak of Agrippa only in relationship to Paul, and we speak of Paul as one whose influence and impact lives on from generation to generation.

14 | Unhindered

Acts 27:1—28:31

George Cafego was a splendid halfback during the early days of professional football. He played for the old Brooklyn Dodgers football team. One day in a game against the New York Giants, Cafego brought the ball upfield practically by himself. Just before the half ended, he broke away over left tackle. First one man hit him, then another, but Cafego kept going. Another man hit him and twisted him around, but Cafego kept going. Finally, about five Giants ganged up on him. Still he plowed goalward. At last he started down, just as the timer's gun exploded. "My soul!" shouted a spectator. "They had to shoot him to stop him!"

As George Cafego could not be stopped, so nothing could hinder the gospel from being proclaimed "in Jerusalem, and in all Judea and Samaria, and even to the remotest part of the earth" (Acts 1:8). The spread of the gospel was unhindered. According to Frank Stagg, that word with which Luke ended the Book of Acts (28:31) is the theme of the book: "unhindered." Stagg said about Luke's purpose in writing Acts, "He writes to show a victory of Christianity—to show the expansion of a concept, the liberation of the gospel as it breaks through barriers that are religious, racial, and national. The author shows how Christianity broke through the narrow limitations which men sought to impose upon it and how it emerged in the liberty which Jesus had given it."[1] Nothing could stop the spread of the gospel. It was unhindered.

Unhindered By Natural Disaster (27:1-44)

This narrative of Paul's trip to Rome is one of the most dramatic and graphic in the book. Notice the technical seaman's terms used in the account. To sail "under the shelter" of an island (vv. 4,7,16) means to come around the south side of the island and use the island for protection from the northern wind. The "Euraquilo" (v. 14) was the name given to the strong northeastern winds which would come sweeping across the waters on the Mediterranean Sea. To "get the ship's boat under control" (v. 16) meant to bring aboard the little dinghy that was usually towed behind the ship. "Undergirding the ship" (v. 17) meant to tighten the cables which were fitted around the hull of the ship with some kind of wench and thus keep the boat from tearing apart in the stormy waters. The "Syrtis" (v. 17) was the quicksand off the African coast. The reference to "neither sun nor stars" (v. 20) was about the heavenly bodies that gave direction to ancient sailors. All of these terms add to the vividness of the account.

Why would Luke devote so much space to the details of this sea journey? Wiersbe made this suggestion: "The major purpose Luke had in mind was the presenting of Paul as the courageous leader who could take command of a difficult situation in a time of great crisis."[2]

Two characters dominate in this account of Paul's journey to Rome: the centurion Julius and the apostle Paul.

1. The Graciousness of the Centurion

Julius belonged to the Augustan cohort (27:1). This was probably a special group of soldiers who acted as liaison officers between Caesar and the Roman provinces. To hold such a position, Julius had to be a man of experience and courage. Yet, he treated Paul with graciousness. When a decision had to be made about setting sail, Paul the prisoner had the chance to express his opinion. Julius did not follow Paul's advice on this occasion, but Paul was allowed the privilege of giving his advice (27:10). Later, when some of the sailors wanted to escape from the ship, Paul told Julius they would die if they left the boat. Immediately, the boat was loosed and allowed to drop into the sea (27:32). If prisoners escaped in Roman days, the guard responsible for them would be killed as punishment. Thus, the Roman soldiers accompanying Paul wanted to kill him and the other prisoners when the boat was in danger. Julius intervened to save Paul (27:43).

Why would this Roman centurion extend such privilege to this Jewish prisoner? Perhaps he recognized in Paul a man of courage and integrity. Perhaps he had heard about the unfair treatment of Paul. For whatever reason, the centurion treated Paul graciously.

2. The Greatness of the Apostle

The most amazing element in the narrative is the fact that Paul is a prisoner, because as the story unfolds Paul dominated every scene. Even though Paul was a prisoner, he nevertheless offered advice and gave direction to the voyage.

We see *Paul's instruction*. When the ship set sail, Paul said, "Men, I perceive that the voyage will certainly be attended with damage and great loss, not only of the cargo and the ship, but also of our lives" (27:10). The "fast" (27:9) was the Day of Atonement, which fell in September or October each year. Sailing was dangerous after September. Paul, the experienced traveler, recommended harboring at Fair Havens. The centurion did not heed Paul's advice, a decision he later regretted.

We see *Paul's revelation*. When the storm came and the ship was in danger, Paul revealed that an angel had spoken to him: "Do not be afraid, Paul; you must stand before Caesar; and behold, God has granted you all those who are sailing with you" (27:24). The sailors had their eyes on the problem. Paul was in touch with the Problem-solver, and he offered a revelation of hope.

We see *Paul's warning*. As the ship came close to shore, some of the sailors tried to escape in a smaller boat that they lowered down the side. Paul warned, "Unless these men remain in the ship, you yourselves cannot be saved" (27:31). By this time, Paul had the attention of the centurion. Thus, the soldiers cut the boat loose, and it fell into the water.

We see *Paul's encouragement*. The storm continued for fourteen days.

By this time, everyone on board was discouraged. So Paul said, "Therefore I encourage you to take some food, for this is for your preservation; for not a hair from the head of any of you shall perish" (27:34). Paul's positive attitude was not based on human circumstances but on divine revelation. Paul did not say, "I'm going to take care of things." He said God is going to take care of things. Positive thinking rooted in divine revelation is a valid attitude for the Christian.

We see *Paul's thanksgiving*. While everyone else was overwhelmed by their problems, Paul was overwhelmed by their blessings. The Bible tells us that Paul "took bread and gave thanks to God in the presence of all" (27:35). Scottish saint Haliburton described thanksgiving as an antidote for discouragement. He said, "When I am in the lowest depths I can pull myself back into the sunshine through the duty of thankfulness."[3] So it was for the apostle Paul. His attitude of gratitude could not be quenched by a storm.

Natural disaster could not stop the spread of the gospel. Despite the storm, the gospel continued "unhindered."

Unhindered By Physical Affliction (28:1-10)

Paul survived his crisis on the sea only to be faced by another crisis on the land. The Bible tells us, "Thus it happened that they all were brought safely to land" (27:44). Malta was their island of refuge. The natives treated Paul and the others with "extraordinary kindness" (28:2). Did Luke intend this reference to be a stab at the enemies of Paul? The Jews, who considered themselves civilized, treated Paul with animosity. The natives, who were considered uncivilized, treated Paul with brotherly kindness. Kindness was not the primary focus of Luke's account, however. Luke focused on the physical affliction on the island of Malta.

1. Paul's Affliction (28:1-6)

Paul, always the man of practical concern, busied himself by gathering brushwood for the fire. In one of the bundles was a viper (v. 3). This was perhaps a snake or some other kind of reptile. The natives expected Paul to swell up and die from the bite of the viper. Instead, he merely shook it off and went his way. The God who protected Paul from the storm could also protect him from the bite of a viper.

2. Publius' Affliction (28:7-10)

Publius was "the leading man of the island" (v. 7). Whether that is an official title or a description of Publius is uncertain. Publius' graciousness to Paul was returned in kind with Paul's graciousness to Publius. The father of Publius was ill with a continuing fever. Paul prayed for the man, laid his hands on him, and healed him (v. 8). The God who created the world and sustains it with His power is adequate to give protection from illness and bring healing from illness. Physical affliction could not stop the spread of the gospel. Despite the illness, the gospel continued "unhindered."

Unhindered By Roman Imprisonment (28:11-31)

Finally, the ship carrying Paul landed in Puteoli which was the port of Rome. Being greeted there by some "brethren" (fellow Christians), Paul and his company made their way to Rome. On the way into Rome, they were greeted by other "brethren" (fellow Christians) who had come from Rome to "the Market of Appius," forty-three miles from Rome, and others coming from the "Three Inns" which was thirty-three miles from Rome (v. 15). Luke said these delegations came from Rome "to meet" Paul (v. 15). The Greek word translated "to meet" was used for a deputation which met a general, king, or conqueror. Paul came to Rome as a captive, and he was greeted by the Christian brethren as a conqueror.

However, Paul was not in Rome to bask in the glory of fellowship with Christians, but to witness for the cause of Christ (23:11).

1. The Message Proclaimed to the Jews (28:17-29)

In Rome, Paul was under house arrest. He had a great deal of freedom to meet with other people and to talk about Jesus Christ. The "brethren" in verse 17 is not a reference to fellow Christians but a reference to fellow Jews. After thirty years of opposition by the Jews,

Paul still went to them first with the gospel.

Paul's approach in Rome was similar to the pattern already established. He identified himself with the Jews, saying he had done nothing wrong and that his cause was a fulfillment of "the hope of Israel" (v. 20). He rooted the message in the Old Testament faith, building his message "from both the Law of Moses and from the Prophets" (v. 23). The Jews longed for the establishment of the kingdom of God. Paul explained that the kingdom of God had come in Christ. Always, his message focused on Jesus Christ: who He was, what He had done, and what He would do.

How did the Jews in Rome respond? They responded in the same way Jews responded to Paul in every city of the Roman world. Some believed, and some did not. Again, the key issue was the universality of the gospel. The gospel was not just for the Jews but for all who would believe in Jesus as the Christ. Even though this universal application of the gospel was predicted in the Jewish prophets (vv. 25-27), the Jews in Rome would not accept it. The Bible tells us, "When he had spoken these words, the Jews departed, having a great dispute among themselves" (v. 29). They disbelieved, they disputed, and then they departed.

2. The Message Proclaimed to the Gentiles (28:30-31)

Luke, who at times would spend several verses on a conversation lasting only a few minutes, now summarized two years in one verse. Luke said, "He stayed two full years in his rented quarters, and was welcoming all who came to him" (v. 30). What happened during these two years?

These two years were *productive years* for Paul. During the time Paul not only built up the church at Rome, but he also wrote Colossians, Philemon, Philippians, and Ephesians which are some of the richest books in the New Testament. These Epistles have provided spiritual sustenance and enlightenment to Christians throughout the centuries.

These two years were also *witnessing years* for Paul. Paul's testimony in Philippians 1:13 is that his bonds were known throughout the entire praetorian guard. Paul was under guard twenty-four hours a day and was in chains (Acts 28:20; Eph. 6:20). The Greek word is *halusis* which means a short length of chain connecting the wrist of the prisoner with the wrist of the guard. The praetorian guard was made up of 10,000 elite troops stationed in Rome. So twenty-four hours a day, one after another of these elect soldiers of Rome would be chained to the apostle Paul and forced to be with him all the time. They had to listen to the conversations Paul had with his visitors. They had to listen to him pray. They had to watch as he dictated the Epistles. They had to listen as he retold his conversion experience and challenged them to receive Christ. They had to listen to his "preaching the kingdom of God, and teaching concerning the Lord Jesus Christ" (v. 31). These soldiers were Paul's captive audience as he witnessed about Christ. His imprisonment provided the opportunity for the gospel to penetrate into the ranks of the most powerful men of the world. Despite Paul's imprisonment, the gospel continued "unhindered."

Luke concluded his book without informing us about the ultimate end of Paul because that was not his purpose. The Book of Acts was not a book about Paul. It was a book about the spread of the gospel. Luke's purpose was to show the gradual spread of Christianity against all odds. The proclamation of the gospel under the sovereignty of God will continue until all the world hears the message. Nothing or nobody can stop it, "for the Lord God omnipotent reigneth" (Rev. 19:6, KJV). When we realize that truth in the same way the apostle Paul did, then, like him and the other Christians in the Book of Acts, we can begin *living expectantly!*

Notes

Chapter 1

1. Paul W. Powell, *The Saint Peter Principle* (Nashville: Broadman Press, 1982), 54.
2. G. Campbell Morgan, *Great Chapters of the Bible* (New York: Fleming H. Revell, 1935), 223.
3. Warren Wiersbe, *Be Dynamic* (Wheaton, Ill.: Victor Books, 1987), 27.

Chapter 2

1. Gipsy Smith, *Gipsy Smith's Best Sermons as Delivered in Brooklyn* (New York: J. S. Ogilvie, 1907), 242.
2. J. C. Pollock, *Moody* (New York: The Macmillan Co., 1963), 162.
3. William Barclay, *The Acts of the Apostles* (Philadelphia: The Westminster Press, 1953), 26.

Chapter 3

1. F. F. Bruce, *The Book of Acts* (Grand Rapids, Mich.: William B. Eerdmans, 1954), 84.
2. William M. Pinson, Jr., *Applying the Gospel* (Nashville: Broadman Press, 1975), 17.
3. Barclay, 39.
4. W. Graham Scroggie, *The Acts of the Apostles* (Grand Rapids, Mich.: Zondervan Publishing House, 1976), 45.

Chapter 4

1. Jerry Gunnells, "Looking for the 'Real,' " a sermon preached at Springhill Baptist Church, Mobile, Alabama, February 21, 1982.
2. Jay Cannon, *Celebrate Yourself* (Waco: Word, 1977), 123-24.
3. Barclay, 48.
4. Quoted in Dwight L. Carson, *Run and Not be Weary* (Old Tappan, N.J.: Fleming H. Revell, 1974), 141.
5. Lewis A. Drummond, "The Essence of Effective Evangelism," *Pulpit Digest*, March-April 1983, 39-40.
6. Mark Trotter, "Is Jesus for Everyone?" *Pulpit Digest*, July-August 1978, 14.

Chapter 5

1. Lyle E. Schaller, *Getting Things Done* (Nashville: Abingdon Press, 1986), 210.

2. Gary R. Collins, *The Magnificent Mind* (Waco: Word, 1985), 95-96.

3. Harold E. Buell, "Is Your Bag Packed for Eternity?" *Pulpit Digest*, January-February 1978, 51.

4. Jill Morgan, *A Man of the Word* (Grand Rapids, Mich.: Baker, 1972), 216.

5. Tim Hansel, *Holy Sweat* (Waco: Word, 1987), 141.

6. James E. McReynolds, *America's No. 1 Drug Problem* (Nashville: Broadman Press, 1977), 112.

Chapter 6

1. Wiersbe, 87.

2. Barclay, 70.

Chapter 7

1. Arthur Porritt, *John Henry Jowett* (George H. Doran Co., 1924), 238.

2. Bruce, 296.

3. Barclay, 71.

4. James E. Carter, *Following Jesus* (Nashville: Broadman Press, 1977), 114.

5. Donald E. Demaray, *Pulpit Giants: What Makes Them Great* (Chicago: Moody Press, 1973), 55.

6. R. L. Middleton, *My Cup Runneth Over* (Nashville: Broadman Press, 1960), 60.

7. James W. Cox, ed., *The Minister's Manual, 1984* (San Francisco: Harper, 1984), 50-51.

8. *The Best of Vance Havner* (Grand Rapids, Mich.: Baker, 1969), 21-23.

Chapter 8

1. Bruce, 215.

2. Tom Kelly, ed., *Quote: Speaker's Digest* 65 (Los Cruces, N.Mex.: Cheallaigh Shamrock, 1973), 551.

Chapter 9

1. F. F. Bruce, *Commentary on the Book of Acts* (Grand Rapids, Mich.: William B. Eerdmans, 1956), 238.

2. W. E. Sangster, *Power in Preaching* (Grand Rapids, Mich.: Baker, 1958), 30-32.

3. Barclay, 94.

4. Cecil G. Osborne, *The Art of Becoming a Whole Person* (Waco: Word, 1978), 51.

5. Emil Brunner, *The Word and the World*, 2nd ed. (New York: Charles Scribner's Sons, 1932), 108.

6. John R. W. Stott, *Christian Mission in the Modern World* (Downers Grove, Ill.: Intervarsity Press, 1975), 38 *ff.*

Chapter 10

1. James E. Carter, *People Parables* (Grand Rapids, Mich.: Baker, 1973), 47.

2. Scroggie, 119.

Chapter 11
1. E. Stanley Jones, *A Song of Ascents* (Nashville: Abingdon Press, 1968), 36.
2. W. Herschel Ford, *Simple Sermons from the Gospel of John*, vol. 2 (Grand Rapids, Mich.: Zondervan Press, 1958), 223.
3. T. C. Smith, "Acts" in *The Broadman Bible Commentary*, vol. 10 (Nashville: Broadman Press, 1970), 102.
4. George Gallup, Jr. and David Poling, *The Search for American's Faith* (Nashville: Abingdon Press, 1980), 42.

Chapter 12
1. Jones, 117.
2. Lloyd John Ogilvie, *You've Got Charisma!* (New York: Abingdon Press, 1975), 18.
3. Lloyd John Ogilvie, *Drumbeat of Love* (Waco: Word, 1976), 246.

Chapter 13
1. Tom Kelly, ed., *Quote: Speaker's Digest* 82 (Los Cruces, N.Mex.: Cheallaigh Shamrock, 1982), 50.
2. Bruce, 492.

Chapter 14
1. Frank Stagg, *The Book of Acts* (Nashville: Broadman Press, 1955), 12.
2. Warren Wiersbe, *Be Daring* (Wheaton, Ill.: Victor Books, 1988), 141-42.
3. Donald Macleod, "Bring God into Thankfulness," *Pulpit Digest*, September-October 1984, 54.

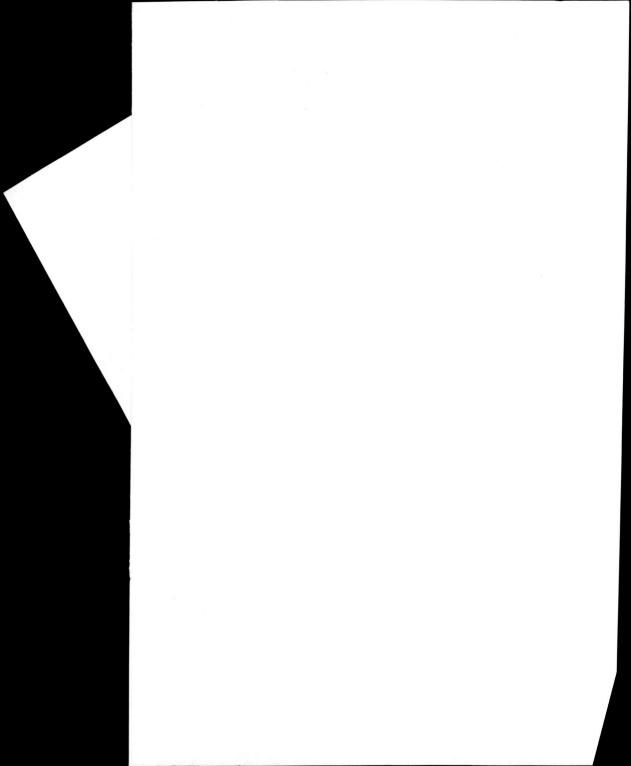

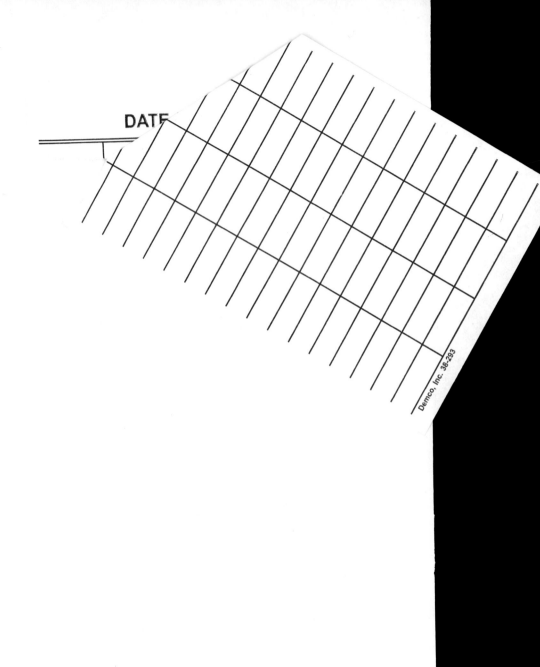

DATE

Demco, Inc. 38-293